Walk in
LIGHT
in This World of
DARKNESS

Katrina D. Stanley

Trilogy Christian Publishers

A Wholly Owned Subsidiary of Trinity Broadcasting Network

2442 Michelle Drive

Tustin, CA 92780

Copyright © 2024 by Katrina D. Stanley

For information, address Trilogy Christian Publishing

Rights Department, 2442 Michelle Drive, Tustin, Ca 92780.

Trilogy Christian Publishing/ TBN and colophon are trademarks of Trinity Broadcasting Network.

For information about special discounts for bulk purchases, please contact Trilogy Christian Publishing.

Trilogy Disclaimer: The views and content expressed in this book are those of the author and may not necessarily reflect the views and doctrine of Trilogy Christian Publishing or the Trinity Broadcasting Network.

10 9 8 7 6 5 4 3 2 1
Library of Congress Cataloging-in-Publication Data is available.
ISBN 979-8-89041-853-1
ISBN 979-8-89041-854-8 (ebook)

Then I heard the voice of the Lord saying, "Whom shall I send? And who will go for us?"

And I said, "Here am I. Send me!"

Isaiah 6:8 (NIV)

Dedication

To my children, Tabitha and Aaron—God gave me life through giving life to you. You are the reason I never gave up. Stand for truth, even if it means you stand alone—know that with God, you never stand alone. Never give up. There is always hope. We've only just begun!

To my mother, whose love, strength, and wisdom guided me into the truth that makes me who I am today. I love you more than I can say.

To my family, whose unconditional love and laughter keep us afloat during the floods—there's no place like home.

To Joy Webb, who has been a true friend since the beginning. Whether sunshine or rain your friendship remains, for which I will forever cherish.

To Alisa Burack, whose countless hours of listening, praying, and speaking God's truth gave me the strength to hold onto the hope of a brighter tomorrow. A truer friend cannot otherwise be found.

To Debbie Gooding, who was willing to listen to the still small voice for the "season" of connecting with me daily to ensure I did not face my journey on uncharted waters alone. I am forever grateful.

To Shelley Persinger, who is a champion for the faith in Christ Jesus. In my darkest moments, you never left my side. You embody being like Christ. Your spirit is life-giving. Ministry with you is pure, seeking after the Father's heart. You have made a forever imprint in my heart.

To Carol Bogle, whose compassion, hospitality, and encouragement showed me the light that helped me to keep on keeping on. The light in your eyes, the smile on your face, and the love in your heart speak Jesus in everything you do.

To my pastors, who could see what God sees in me—Thank you!

Faith is never giving up your dream and being determined to believe you will one day achieve it.

Table of Contents

Foreword

Katrina Stanley and I met over ten years ago. I have had the privilege of watching and interacting with a woman of God who truly wants to see God's people delivered from the darkness of ignorance.

Ephesians 5:11 (NKJV) instructs us, "and have no fellowship with the unfruitful works of darkness, but rather expose *them*," and Ephesians 5:13 (NKJV) states, "but all things that are exposed are made manifest by the light, for whatever makes manifest is light."

Katrina Stanley Ministries is a light bearer. She writes about those things she has learned, but even more importantly, what she has experienced. I have watched her firsthand walk through many a valley and never saw her falter from that which the Holy Spirit gave her. I believe this book is to be underlined, highlighted, meditated on, prayed over, and read again and again. This little book is meat for the soul. I recommend *Walk in His Light in This World of Darkness* for any serious student of the Word of God. Make room for it in your library.

—Shelley Cramer Persinger

Introduction

The world we live in today is complex, and knowledge is vast with the many different cultures among us. In the midst of so many uncertainties, the quest for knowledge and the pursuit of happiness is profound among the masses. There are religions in this world that will greatly support the belief that God is indeed the supreme Ruler of all, but they say that having a personal relationship with Him is not possible, that a close relationship with the one who can send a person to hell is simply unattainable, and that the only way one can get to heaven is by doing more good than bad.

Maybe you are a person who has "tried that church stuff before" but ended up wounded or disillusioned. Perhaps you are a new Christian wondering what to expect. We all have the need for a deep satisfaction in our souls that will give us meaning in our lives. We have all pondered the question, "What is the purpose of my life?" Many have found it, and many never will.

We can face struggles that seem so impossible to overcome that we look up to heaven and ask, 'Are you there?'[1] There are simple, basic truths we need to understand and put in place to live a life of victory in this world of darkness. This book will look at these truths.

Chapter 1

Get Knowledge and Obtain Understanding

Buy the truth and do not sell it—

wisdom, instruction and insight as well.

Proverbs 23:23, NIV

Understanding the Need for a Savior

With all the information present in this world, one might have a difficult time sifting through the many ideas, thoughts, and belief systems. Many have spent years searching through great teachings in our history, trying to discover the answers that will explain our current condition. There is no lack of spiritual debate to explain the purpose of our existence. Yet, deep inside each of us, deep within our souls, we long for more.

What will satisfy the need for understanding this great mystery? What must we comprehend to unlock the deep spiritual truths and mysteries to bring salvation to our human condition—to our souls? The answers to these questions and more are found in the Creator—the source of life. Within Him lies inexhaustible knowledge and wisdom that will satisfy the long and sought-after quest to the need for a Savior.

To understand the need for a Savior, we must understand who we are as a person. What makes us who we are? We have a mind able to think and comprehend, a soul that is the sum of our personality, will, and emotions developed by life experiences, as well as a spirit, which is the part of us that gives life.

In the beginning, in Genesis 1:27, we find we are created in God's image, His likeness. We are imprinted with His characteristics mentally, emotionally, and socially. Mentally, we can reason and choose, which reflects God's intellect and ability to choose. Emotionally, we have the ability to feel just as God is able to feel. God showed His wrath by flooding the earth because of sin. God kept His promise to deliver the Israelites by freeing them from slavery in Egypt. In addition, He showed compassion to the Israelites by feeding and clothing them while they wandered in the wilderness. Socially, man was created for fellowship, which represents God's nature and His love. We are made this way to be in fellowship with Him. God made a promise to man and planned from the beginning to provide all that mankind would ever need to live well on this earth and stay in close fellowship with Him. In the beginning, God walked and talked with Adam daily, just like two friends talk with each other on a regular basis. As God walked with Adam, He guided him in what He wanted him to do.

When God said, "It is not good for man to be alone" (Genesis 2:18, NLV), He created a woman for Adam. Life in the garden of Eden was pure, perfect, and peaceful because God's presence was there. Even though Adam and Eve were unclothed, they did not feel shame. Like small children, their eyes were not opened to their bodies being unclothed, and they perceived nothing wrong with it.

God told Adam and Eve to take care of everything in the garden. He told them they could eat anything in the garden except fruit from the tree of knowledge of good and evil. God told them that if they ate this fruit, they would surely die. As we read in Genesis 3, the serpent, who is described as the craftiest of all the wild animals God made, set the ultimate trap for Eve. He convinced her she would not die if she ate the fruit from the tree of knowledge of good and evil, but instead, she would become like God and know everything, both good and evil. So, Eve convinced herself that this was a good idea, and she ate the fruit. She offered it to Adam, who also ate the fruit.

At that moment, Adam and Eve's eyes were opened. For the first time, they realized they were naked and suddenly felt shame at their nakedness. They did not immediately die a physical death; however, as a result of their disobedience, they brought on themselves the curse of sin that would lead to death through separation from God. This curse of sin would plague all mankind from then on, every generation yet to be, which is why this one act of disobedience is called the fall of man. Their sin of disobedience caused them to be separated from God. This separation caused the light of God's presence to be removed from their inward being. From that point on, they were subjected to living in this world without having the internal hope of eternal fellowship with God.

This one moment in time caused all mankind to be born with what is called a sin nature. The natural disposition to sin against God is born into our nature—before we are given the opportunity to do anything.

From the beginning, God knew the plans He had for us, plans for good and not harm, plans for a future with hope, as stated in Jeremiah 29:11. No matter how we choose to dress ourselves, God sees us as we are. He knows everything about us (Psalm 139:16).

From the beginning, God made provision to save mankind from sin and death. He knew that, no matter how hard we tried to follow the rules to live by, we would not be able to keep all of them all the time. According to James 2:10, a person who makes one mistake is as guilty as the person who has broken all the rules. In a simple math equation, when a negative number is multiplied by a positive number, the end result will always be a negative number. If we commit one sin, we will earn the wages of that sin, which is death. God's plan was to send His only Son, Jesus Christ, into this world to pay the price required to free us from the curse of sin and death.

God saves us by His power and His love. He gives faith to believe. Salvation is not earned by good deeds or by sacrifices, regardless of how sincere the person is. We are saved by grace through faith. It is a gift from God and not of our own works, so no one can boast about their own efforts (Ephesians 2:8–9).

God created us in His image. He created us to have fellowship with Him. In addition, He created us with a purpose He planned for us long before we were born. God knows we need Him. God put within us a desire to be more than we are, to accomplish more than we can accomplish, and to understand greater than we can comprehend. Only God can satisfy the longing within us to know who we are and our purpose. Some call this a God-shaped hole, and only God can fill this void. Unfortunately, many go through their lives never understanding this and look for other things to fill this void.

Understanding Who God Really Is

God tells us that we are destroyed because we don't
know Him (Hosea 4:6). In my struggle to overcome my
difficult past, a dear friend encouraged me to go to the
Father. Taking this step meant I had to change my view
of God. It was easy to see God as one who cast down
punishment for making a mistake—this I had become
familiar with in my life. Allowing myself to go to God as a
father, someone I could not see or touch, while knowing He
is perfect and I am not, was a real challenge for me. I was
guarded with whom I allowed myself to trust. How do you
trust what you cannot see? By faith. Pleasing God requires
faith. Before you can come to Him, you must believe He
is the one true God and that He will answer you when you
call on Him (Hebrews 11:6).

There are many terms to describe who God is. God is
holy. God is righteous. God is perfect. He is faithful and
just in all He does (Deuteronomy 32:4). He is perfect in
every way, and we are measured by His standard, not ours.

God rules in righteousness and will give to each person according to what a person does (Romans 2:6). God cannot look at sin. In fact, sin in the world got so bad at one point, God flooded the entire earth, and everyone living at the time died, except Noah and his family, because they would not turn away from their sin and turn to God. Noah and his family were the only people on earth God found to be living the way He commanded.

God is love. God showed how much He loved us by sending His only Son into the world so that we might have eternal life through Him. This is real love (1 John 4:8–9). God's love for us does not depend on us. God is love. Since He is perfect and we are not, what makes Him interested in us? (Psalm 8:4). He planned from the beginning to adopt us into His family, and this gave Him much pleasure (Ephesians 1:4–5). Adoption into God's family is only possible through accepting the love Jesus Christ showed for us through His death on the cross of Calvary. There is no other way to come to God who is in heaven (John 14:6). Give thanks to the Lord, for He is good; He is faithful forever (Jeremiah 33:11).

One name of God is Jehovah Jireh. In Hebrew, this means "provider" (Genesis 22:14). Even after Adam and Eve disobeyed God, He showed His love for them in that He provided clothing to cover their nakedness. While growing up, I watched my parents work to provide what we needed to be healthy and well cared for—physically, emotionally, and spiritually. It was not until I was an adult that I realized my parents did not depend on themselves to provide these things to us. They depended on God for what they needed. They learned God was their source, their provider, and through their dependence on Him and asking God to provide what they needed, we received God's provision. The same is true for us. When we depend on Jesus Christ for our salvation, we receive all God has for us, and the world around us can receive from that as well (Philippians 4:19).

God is omniscient. God knows everything. He reveals deep and mysterious things and knows what lies hidden in darkness. For He is surrounded by light (Daniel 2:22). God watches how people live; He sees everything they do (Job 34:21). "The Lord looks down from heaven and sees the whole human race. From his throne he observes all who live on the earth. He made their hearts, so he understands everything they do" (Psalm 33:13–15, NLT). "You know when I sit down or stand up. You know my thoughts even when I'm far away. You see me when I travel and when I rest at home. You know everything I do" (Psalm 139:2–3, NLT). God knows the final hour of existence on this earth for all mankind. "However, no one knows the day or hour when these things will happen, not even the angels in heaven or the Son himself. Only the Father knows" (Matthew 24:36, NLT).

God is omnipresent. God is present everywhere.

> I can never escape from your spirit! I can never get away from your presence! If I go up to heaven, you are there; if I go down to the grave, you are there. If I ride the wings of the morning, if I dwell by the farthest oceans, even there your hand will guide me, and your strength will support me.
>
> Psalm 139:7–10 (NLT)

"'Can anyone hide from me in a secret place? Am I not everywhere in all the heavens and earth?' says the Lord" (Jeremiah 23:24, NLT). "Nothing in all creation is hidden from God. Everything is naked and exposed before his eyes, and he is the one to whom we are accountable" (Hebrews 4:13, NLT). God is everywhere all the time. He is with us wherever we are even if we do not realize it.

God is omnipotent. God is all-powerful. "O Lord God! You have made the heavens and earth by your great power; nothing is too hard for you!" (Jeremiah 32:17, TLB). "Have you never heard? Have you never understood? The Lord is the everlasting God, the Creator of all the earth. He never grows weak or weary. No one can measure the depths of his understanding" (Isaiah 40:28, NLT). With God, everything is possible (Matthew 19:26). "For God says, 'I will break the strength of the wicked, but I will increase the power of the godly'" (Psalm 75:10, NLT).

God is holy. God rules with justice and mercy.

> But the Lord reigns forever, executing judgment from his throne. He will judge the

world with justice and rule the nations with fairness. The Lord is a shelter for the oppressed, a refuge in times of trouble. Those who know your name trust in you, for you, O Lord, do not abandon those who search for you.

Psalm 9:7–10 (NLT)

"So don't you think God will surely give justice to his chosen people who cry out to him day and night? Will he keep putting them off?" (Luke 18:7, NLT). "For the Lord God is our sun and our shield. He gives us grace and glory. The Lord will withhold no good thing from those who do what is right" (Psalm 84:11, NLT), but "the wicked will be removed from the land, and the treacherous will be uprooted" (Proverbs 2:22, NLT). "For the Lord loves justice and fairness; he will never abandon his people" (Psalm 37:28, TLB).

"He showed you these things so you would know that the Lord is God and there is no other…So remember this and keep it firmly in mind: The Lord is God both in heaven and on earth, and there is no other" (Deuteronomy

4:35, 39, NLT). "I am the God of your Father—the God of Abraham, the God of Isaac, and the God of Jacob" (Exodus 3:6, NLT). "God replied to Moses, 'I AM WHO I AM'" (Exodus 3:14, NLT).

God is the one true God. "I am the Lord; there is no other God. I have equipped you for battle, though you don't even know me" (Isaiah 45:5, NLT). "'I am the Alpha and the Omega—the beginning and the end,' says the Lord God. 'I am the One who is, who always was, and who is still to come—The Almighty One'" (Revelation 1:8, NLT). "Holy, holy, holy is the Lord God, the Almighty—the one who always was, who is, and who is still to come" (Revelation 4:8, NLT).

"The Lord is good to everyone. He showers compassion on all his creation" (Psalm 145:9, NLT). "O Lord, you are so good, so ready to forgive, so full of unfailing love for all who ask for your help" (Psalm 86:5, NLT). "Give thanks to the Lord, for he is good! His faithful love endures forever" (1 Chronicles 16:34, NLT). God is God, and God is good.

Who We Are Without God

God tells us because we are His creation, we have the built-in ability to recognize God's existence.

> But God shows his anger from heaven against all sinful, wicked people who suppress the truth by their wickedness. They know the truth about God because he has made it obvious to them. For ever since the world was created, people have seen the earth and sky. Through everything God made, they can clearly see his invisible qualities—his eternal power and divine nature. So they have no excuse for not knowing God.
>
> Yes, they knew God, but they wouldn't worship him as God or even give him thanks. And they began to think up foolish ideas of what God was like. As a result, their minds became dark and confused.

Romans 1:18–21 (NLT)

The original sin has taken its toll on this world we live in, and mankind has since been in a struggle to overcome the darkness in this world. "Then the Lord said, 'I have seen how stubborn and rebellious these people are'" (Exodus 32:9, NLT). "I know, Lord, that our lives are not our own. We are not able to plan our own course" (Jeremiah 10:23, NLT). God, in His infinite wisdom and mercy, gives us the rules we need to live by. "This Book of the Law shall not depart from your mouth, but you shall meditate on it day and night, so that you may be careful to do according to all that is written in it. For then you will make your way prosperous, and then you will have good success" (Joshua 1:8, ESV).

In our feeble attempt to submit to God, we are unable to achieve this on our own. "The human heart is the most deceitful of all things, and desperately wicked. Who really knows how bad it is?" (Jeremiah 17:9, NLT). But because of God's infinite mercy, He warns us of impending judgment, and He sends His prophets to tell us how we have gone astray. God said, "Go and tell this people: 'Yes, you hear, but you don't understand. You certainly see, but you don't get the point!'" (Isaiah 6:9, CJB). God promises us that if we are willing and obedient, we will receive the good of the land (Isaiah 1:19). "What is more pleasing to the Lord: your burnt offerings and sacrifices or your obedience to his voice?" (1 Samuel 15:22, NLT). Obedience and listening to God are far more rewarding than offering the biggest and best sacrifice a person could make.

"We are all infected and impure with sin. When we display our righteous deeds, they are nothing but filthy rags. Like autumn leaves, we wither and fall, and our sins sweep us away like the wind" (Isaiah 64:6, NLT). So God made provision to save us from the eternal doom of sin, and God, who cannot lie, did what He had planned to do from the beginning (Numbers 23:19). "For this is how God loved the world: He gave his one and only Son, so that everyone who believes in him will not perish but have eternal life" (John 3:16, NLT). We make mistakes and are in need of a Savior (Romans 3:23).

> For God presented Jesus as the sacrifice for sin. People are made right with God when they believe that Jesus sacrificed his life, shedding his blood. This sacrifice shows that God was being fair when he held back and did

not punish those who sinned in times past, for he was looking ahead and including them in what he would do in this present time. God did this to demonstrate his righteousness, for he himself is fair and just, and he makes sinners right in his sight when they believe in Jesus.

Romans 3:25–26 (NLT)

Abraham was a man God called the first Hebrew. He was chosen by God to be the father of the nation of Israel. He was the one whom God chose to establish the covenant agreement to bring forth a Savior, not only to the Jewish people but also to the people of the world. Abraham believed God, so God declared him to be righteous (Genesis 15:6). When people work, their wages are not a gift. Workers earn what they receive. But people are declared righteous because of their faith, not because of their work (Romans 4:4–5). "If you belong to Christ, then you are Abraham's seed, and heirs according to the promise" (Galatians 3:29, NIV).

"The wages of sin is death, but the free gift of God is

eternal life through Jesus Christ our Lord" (Romans 6:23, TLB).

> If you openly declare that Jesus is Lord and believe in your heart that God raised him from the dead, you will be saved. For it is by believing in your heart that you are made right with God, and it is by openly declaring your faith that you are saved. As the Scriptures tell us, "Anyone who trusts in him will never be disgraced."

Romans 10:9–11 (NLT)

"Everyone who calls on the name of the Lord will be saved" (Romans 10:13, NLT). "God saved you by his grace when you believed. And you can't take credit for this; it is a gift from God" (Ephesians 2:8, NLT).

> Therefore, since we have been made right in God's sight by faith, we have peace with God because of what Jesus Christ our Lord has done for us. Because of our faith, Christ has brought us into this place of undeserved privilege

where we now stand, and we confidently and joyfully look forward to sharing God's glory.

Romans 5:1–2 (NLT)

"Everyone who believes in him will have eternal life" (John 3:15, NLT). No matter how hard we try, we will never measure up to God's standard of right on our own. We make mistakes every day. We need God's provision for a reconciled relationship with Him. We all need a Savior. We all need Jesus. Jesus is our only hope.

Who God Says We Are as Christians

A covenant is a promise, a contract, or a binding agreement between two parties. Once we become Christians, God no longer sees us in our original sin state. He sees us covered by His Son, Jesus. We become clothed in the robes of righteousness—Jesus becomes our righteousness. "Take off his filthy clothes...See, I have taken away your sins, and now I am giving you these fine new clothes" (Zechariah 3:4, NLT). "This means that anyone who belongs to Christ has become a new person. The old life is gone; a new life has begun!" (2 Corinthians 5:17, NLT). Through Jesus shedding His blood, God has made a covenant with us. By accepting the atoning sacrifice Jesus Christ made for us on the cross of Calvary, we make a covenant with God—a covenant that means God is forever on our side, and we are forever called a child of God. "But to all who believed him and accepted him, he gave the right to become children of God" (John 1:12, NLT). From this point forward, when God looks at us, He no longer sees us in the filthy rags of sin—He sees His Son, Jesus. "The Spirit of God, who raised Jesus from the dead, lives in you" (Romans 8:11, NLT). "But in fact, Christ has been raised from the dead. He is the first of a great harvest of all who have died. So you see, just as death came into the world through a man, now the resurrection from the dead has begun through another man" (1 Corinthians 15:20–21, NLT). "For just as the Father gives life to those he raises from the dead, so the Son gives life to anyone he wants" (John 5:21, NLT). Romans 10:13 tells us all who call on the name of Jesus will be saved.

When we become Christians, God's Holy Spirit takes up residence in our hearts and gives us new life. We are saved from the curse of sin and death. A seal is an official mark of identification. When we become Christians, we are sealed by the Holy Spirit. "[He] set his seal of ownership on us, and put his Spirit in our hearts as a deposit, guaranteeing what is to come" (2 Corinthians 1:22, NIV). The seal of God's Spirit signifies security, authenticity, ownership, and authority. "I give them eternal life, and they shall never perish; no one will snatch them out of my hand" (John 10:28, NIV). When our human spirit is joined with God's Holy Spirit, we are regenerated—made new. Our human spirit becomes one with God's Holy Spirit and is perfect. We have within us divine, eternal life that gives us new life. Our spirit agrees with the Spirit of God that we are God's children. We have the hope of eternal life through Christ in us.

> For God's will was for us to be made holy by the sacrifice of the body of Jesus Christ, once for all time. Under the old covenant, the priest stands and ministers before the altar day

after day, offering the same sacrifices again and again, which can never take away sins. But our High Priest [Jesus] offered himself to God as a single sacrifice for sins, good for all time. Then he sat down in the place of honor at God's right hand.

Hebrews 10:10–12 (NLT)

As Christians, we are holy because God's Holy Spirit, who lives within us, is holy. "But now you must be holy in everything you do, just as God who chose you is holy" (1 Peter 1:15, NLT).

As people who are made new through Jesus Christ, Jesus becomes our advocate and intercedes for us day and night. "He is able to save completely all who come to God through him. Since he will live forever, he will always be there to remind God that he has paid for their sins with his blood" (Hebrews 7:25, TLB). We become a friend of God: "I no longer call you slaves, because a master doesn't confide in his slaves. Now you are my friends, since I have told you everything the Father told me" (John 15:15, NLT). We are His representative on this earth: "But you are a chosen people, a royal priesthood, a holy nation, God's special possession, that you may declare the praises of him who called you out of darkness into his wonderful light" (1 Peter 2:9, NIV). "For they are your people—your special possession" (1 Kings 8:51, NLT). As Christians, we are a child of God. The object of His love and compassion, the apple of His eye, His very heartbeat.

> God saved you by his grace when you believed. And you can't take credit for this; it is a gift from God. Salvation is not a reward for the good things we have done, so none of us can boast about it. For we are God's masterpiece. He has created us anew in Christ Jesus, so we can do the good things he planned for us long ago.
>
> Ephesians 2:8–10 (NLT)

We are covered by God's grace and called to be a witness to this world that God's love is unconditional and will make us complete. "Throw off your old sinful nature and your former way of life, which is corrupted by lust and deception. Instead, let the Spirit renew your thoughts and attitudes. Put on your new nature, created to be like God—truly righteous and holy" (Ephesians 4:22–24, NLT). Putting on a new nature is the process of sanctification or being set apart as holy and sacred or the process of becoming more like Christ Jesus every day. We are saved by grace, which means we cannot earn it. We cannot become more like Christ on our own. We must allow the Holy Spirit to work in us to change us into the likeness of Christ. The Lord rewards us for doing good and being faithful (1 Samuel 26:23). When God is for us, who can be against us? (Romans 8:31). Purpose in your heart to go forward to finish the course God has laid out for you to receive the reward God has for you (Philippians 3:14). God tells us over and over He will never leave us or forsake us. He tells us over and over not to be afraid and not to get discouraged because God will help us and strengthen us (Deuteronomy 31:6, Isaiah 41:10). "Overwhelming victory is ours through Christ, who loved us" (Romans 8:37, NLT). God is our refuge and strength, always ready to help in times of need (Psalm 46:1).[2]

Walk in Wisdom

God tells us that with knowledge, we get understanding and use wisdom. Do not forget or turn away from His words. We have a better understanding of our need for a Savior, a better understanding of God and who we are as Christians. However, we now must put what we have learned into action. We do this using wisdom.

> If you need wisdom, ask our generous God, and he will give it to you. He will not rebuke you for asking. But when you ask him, be sure that your faith is in God alone. Do not waver, for a person with divided loyalty is as unsettled as a wave of the sea that is blown and tossed by the wind.

> James 1:5–6 (NLT)

So Christ has really set us free. "Now make sure that you stay free, and don't get tied up again in slavery to the law" (Galatians 5:1, NLT). God wants us to live in such a way everyone will see the change He made in our lives by how we live, what we say, and what we do.

In the Old Testament, God gave guidelines to live by, which are called the Ten Commandments. God knew we would never be able to fully abide by these laws on our own. Galatians 5:1 tells us that now we are Christians, we are to purpose in our hearts to live a life that would show the world we are God's children. The Ten Commandments give us guidelines to live by. Walking in a relationship with Christ gives us the ability to successfully live within these guidelines because the Holy Spirit within us guides us and helps us make the choices necessary to adhere to these guidelines.

In addition to fellowship with Him, God created us to reach the world with His message of love, grace, and mercy. Then Jesus came to them and said,

> I have been given all authority in heaven and on earth. Therefore, go and make disciples of all the nations, baptizing them in the name of the Father and the Son and the Holy Spirit.

Teach these new disciples to obey all the commands I have given you. And be sure of this: I am with you always, even to the end of the age.

Matthew 28:18–20 (NLT)

God tells us to love Him and love our neighbor as ourselves (Mark 12:30–31). Colossians 2:2–4 tells us He wants us to be knit together by strong ties of love and to understand God's plan, which is Christ Himself. Within Him, you will find all the treasures of wisdom and knowledge.

Jesus said, "I am the way, the truth, and the life. No one can come to the Father [God] except through me" (John 14:6, NLT). Jesus is life to our souls. A life without Jesus is like someone who has asthma and is gasping for the breath of air that will save them. Without the proper intervention and treatment, they will die. The same is true of Jesus. Without Him, there is no intervention to forgive sin and give eternal life in heaven. With knowledge, obtain understanding and use wisdom to walk in the light of His salvation.

Time of Reflection

For we are the temple of the living God. As God said: "I will live in them and walk among them. I will be their God, and they will be my people."

2 Corinthians 6:16 (NLT)

How would you describe your relationship with God?

List three things you learned about God and having a relationship with him.

1.

2.

3.

Recall a time in your life when God made Himself real to you during a time when you felt alone.

What does using wisdom mean to you?

Take a moment to pray and ask the Lord to draw you closer to Him and give you an increase in knowledge, understanding, and wisdom in your walk with Him.

Chapter 2

A Willing Spirit

Restore to me the joy of your salvation and grant me a willing spirit, to sustain me.

Psalm 51:12 (NIV)

Willingness to Believe

As we discussed in chapter 1, when we become Christians, our human spirit is joined with God's Holy Spirit and at that moment, we become a new person, completely clean and perfect—just as if we never committed even one sin. The process of becoming more like Christ, however, requires a steadfast commitment, one of which will take a lifetime to develop. Let's get started.

"Where there is a will, there's a way" is a saying I grew

up hearing to encourage someone to not give up. God gives each of us our own will. God has a will of His own. He gives us a choice. We all have the ability to believe. For example, when we go to a restaurant to eat, we believe the chairs will hold us up when we sit down, even though we have no evidence on which to base their ability to do so. Before we go to bed at night, we plan what we are going to do the next day, indicating our willingness to believe we will wake up from our night of slumber to do so. For us to walk in all the promises and gifts God has for us, we are told we must have the faith of a child. Then He said, "I tell you the truth, unless you turn from your sins and become like little children, you will never get into the Kingdom of Heaven" (Matthew 18:3, NLT).

When children are very young, they believe what is said as truth. They do not question it. They believe it as "it's just the way it is." God wants us to believe Him with the faith of a little child. He gave each of us a measure of faith (Romans 12:3). Faith in Jesus Christ is required in order to be saved. We are saved by grace through faith. Jesus said, "Truly I tell you, if you have faith as small as a mustard seed, you can say to this mountain, 'Move from here to there,' and it will move. Nothing will be impossible for you" (Matthew 17:20, NIV). Faith gives life to hope. Believing is exercising faith. Exercising faith demonstrates our willingness to believe.

In Mark 9:20–27, we read about a father who brought his son to Jesus to be healed. He told Jesus his son could not speak and had convulsions that threw him to the ground. Jesus asked how long the boy had been like this. The father indicated since his son was very small and said, "'Have mercy on us and help us, if you can.' 'What do you mean, "If I can"?' Jesus asked. 'Anything is possible if a person believes.' The father instantly cried out, 'I do believe, but help me overcome my unbelief!'" (Mark 9:22–24, NLT). Then Jesus commanded the evil spirits to go and never come back, and the boy was healed and stood up. The boy was healed because the boy's father was willing to believe his son could be healed and that Jesus could heal him.

In one of the villages, Jesus met a man with an

advanced case of leprosy. When the man saw
Jesus, he bowed with his face to the ground,
begging to be healed. "Lord," he said, "if you
are willing, you can heal me and make me
clean." Jesus reached out and touched him.
"I am willing," he said. "Be healed!" And
instantly the leprosy disappeared.

Luke 5:12–13 (NLT)

This man was healed because he was willing to exercise
faith to believe by speaking that he knew Jesus could heal
him, and in doing so, he was healed.

Undoubtedly, we have all experienced times of
unbelief. Yet, God says it is impossible to please Him
without believing He can do what He says He will do. Are
you willing to believe all things are possible with God?
God tells us to have faith as a child and not be blinded by
religion or self-imposed expectations. Anyone who trusts in
God will not be disappointed (Romans 10:11).

Chapter 2

Willingness to Accept

"Accept" is a term that means "to come into agreement with something." When a person buys or rents a home, all participants must accept, or come into agreement with, the price and terms of the purchase or lease. As much as God wants His best for us and as much as God has given to us through Christ, we are still required to accept these things into our minds, hearts, and lives. For example, when someone offers you a gift wrapped with a bow, you must be willing to accept this gift, or the person giving it will simply walk away, and you will never know what was offered to you. The same is true of all the gifts God offers His children. Many people never know just how wonderful and powerful these gifts are because they refuse to accept them.

We are given the fruits of the Spirit, which are the attributes of God's character, through His Holy Spirit, who lives in the heart of every believer in Christ—love, joy, peace, patience, kindness, goodness, gentleness, faithfulness, and self-control. These are available to all of God's children and brought to us the moment the Holy

Spirit resides in us. The extent of the fullness of these

gifts operating in our lives is dependent on our willingness

to allow the Lord's transforming power to change us

to become more like Him. When we allow ourselves

to become more like Christ, we treat people with love,

patience, kindness, goodness, and gentleness; we walk

with His peace in the midst of trials; we understand joy can

be found in times of sorrow; we are more faithful in our

promises; and we gain more self-control in what we say

and do. When we become more like Christ, we can say,

"My old self has been crucified with Christ. It is no longer

I who live, but Christ lives in me. So I live in this earthly

body by trusting in the Son of God, who loved me and gave

himself for me" (Galatians 2:20, NLT).

> Now God gives us many kinds of special
> abilities, but it is the same Holy Spirit who
> is the source of them all. There are different
> kinds of service to God, but it is the same Lord
> we are serving. There are many ways in which
> God works in our lives, but it is the same God
> who does the work in and through all of us who

are his. The Holy Spirit displays God's power through each of us as a means of helping the entire church.

To one person the Spirit gives the ability to give wise advice; someone else may be especially good at studying and teaching, and this is his gift from the same Spirit. He gives special faith to another, and to someone else the power to heal the sick. He gives power for doing miracles to some, and to others power to prophesy and preach. He gives someone else the power to know whether evil spirits are speaking through those who claim to be giving God's messages—or whether it is really the Spirit of God who is speaking. Still another person is able to speak in languages he never learned; and others, who do not know the language either, are given power to understand what he is saying. It is the same and only Holy Spirit who gives all these gifts and powers, deciding which each one of us should have.

Our bodies have many parts, but the many parts make up only one body when they are all put together. So it is with the "body" of Christ.

1 Corinthians 12:4–12 (TLB)

These gifts are given to edify and encourage the church and further the kingdom of heaven in each of us. The realization of these gifts requires our willingness to accept them from a loving Father who knows what He wants to accomplish in us and through us. "There are different kinds of gifts, but the same Spirit distributes them. There are different kinds of service, but the same Lord. There are different kinds of working, but in all of them and in everyone it is the same God at work" (1 Corinthians 12:4–6, NIV).

The question now arises: are we willing to accept God's views and His plan and purpose for our lives? A well-known prophet was once asked how he was able to hear God so clearly and able to prophesy with acute accuracy. He said it was because he spent two to three hours alone with God every day, and he surrounded himself with people of like mind and like faith. His ministry helped not only the church but nations around the world to know the heart of God that brought life, hope, and victory to their lives. For his ministry to fulfill God's purpose, he had to be willing to accept God's call on his life and the requirements

God made of him. For him to continue to grow in his relationship with God, he had to be willing to spend time with Him and be obedient to serve God with the unique gifts God gave him. We must be willing to accept God's word as truth for us to see a fulfillment of His truth in our lives. God has a special plan and purpose for each person's life and it will not look the same as anyone else. If we are willing to trust God, He will fulfill His plan in our lives.

Willingness to Receive

As we discussed earlier, a gift is simply a gift if you are not willing to accept it. A song is just a song if you are not willing to sing it, and a good word from the Lord is just a word if you are not willing to receive it and apply it to your life. You can accept a gift given to you, but if you do not unwrap the gift, it remains a gift you willingly accepted but never fully received. The same is true of everything God gives us. If you are willing and obedient, you will receive and enjoy the good things of the land (Isaiah 1:19).

John 4:1–30 tells the story of a woman who was a Samaritan. In verse 10, Jesus said,

"If you only knew the gift God has for you and who you are speaking to, you would ask me, and I would give you living water."

"But sir, you don't have a rope or a bucket," she said, "and this well is very deep. Where would you get this living water? And besides, do you think you're greater than our ancestor Jacob, who gave us this well? How can you offer better water than he and his sons and his animals enjoyed?"

Jesus replied, "Anyone who drinks this water will soon become thirsty again. But those who drink the water I give will never be thirsty again. It becomes a fresh, bubbling spring within them, giving them eternal life."

John 4:10–14 (NLT)

The gifts God gives us produce life in our souls, but we must be willing to receive it.

A person was not feeling well. The doctor gave the diagnosis of cancer. The treatment options were weighed. The risk of becoming sick from the treatment was high, but the risk of the cancer becoming terminal by not receiving the treatment was even higher. The decision was made to receive the treatment. Even though the course of recovery was difficult, this person was healed completely. However, the reality of a life cut short would have been realized if they had not been willing to receive the treatment that brought a cure.

Much like an honored guest who arrives for dinner, unless you open the door and invite them in, you have not received them in your home for dinner. When we realize we need a Savior and we ask Jesus to forgive us, we must still be willing to open the door of our lives and receive Him as our Lord and Savior. When we realize the spiritual gifts God has given us, we must be willing to receive these gifts and allow the Holy Spirit freedom to operate through us. Otherwise, they will be gifts God gave us, but gifts we have never fully received. "When someone has been given much, much will be required in return; and when someone has been entrusted with much, even more will be required" (Luke 12:48, NLT). "Everything we have has come from you, and we give you only what you first gave us" (1 Chronicles 29:14, NLT). Give thanks. God gives us what is good.

Willingness to Surrender

In 2 Samuel 11 and 12, we read the story of King David and Bathsheba. The story tells that King David committed adultery with Bathsheba, the wife of Uriah, while Uriah, a soldier in King David's army, was away fighting in battle. Through this act of adultery, Bathsheba became pregnant. King David knew what he did was wrong, but he was not willing to admit it and accept responsibility. Instead, he went to great lengths to avoid being caught. Unfortunately, this also caused him to be blindsided to confessing his sin before God. As the phrase coined by Sir Walter Scott goes, "What a tangled web we weave, When first we practice to deceive."[3] King David's deceptive practices ultimately cost Uriah his life. Because of David's unwillingness to surrender in obedience to God, first by avoiding the temptation of adultery and then by avoiding confession of his sin, King David brought a curse on himself and his family that included the death of the child Bathsheba gave birth to.

We read in 2 Kings 5 about a valiant soldier named

Naaman who had leprosy. A slave girl spoke of a prophet in Samaria who would pray for God to heal him. Naaman went to see this prophet as it was recommended for him to do. The prophet of God told this soldier of prominence to go to the Jordan River and dip in it seven times, and he would be healed. Naaman became angry, thinking himself worthy of a much more prestigious reception and manner of healing than to go to a muddy river. In fact, he named two preferable places a man of his stature could go to be cleansed. Naaman's servants pleaded with him to obey God, "wash and be cleansed." Finally, Naaman went to the Jordan River and dipped seven times, just as the prophet of God told him to do. Naaman's flesh was restored and became clean like a young boy. When Naaman was willing to surrender his pride for the sake of being healed, he was healed.

We pay a great price when we refuse to surrender to the Lordship of Jesus Christ in our lives. We are human and we will make mistakes. God knows this. But are we willing to humble ourselves and admit our shortcomings to him? "If we confess our sins, he is faithful and just and will forgive us our sins and cleanse us from all unrighteousness" (1 John 1:9, NIV). When we are willing to surrender in obedience to the Lord, we are able to grow in our relationship with Him. "And just as Christ was raised from the dead by the glorious power of the Father, now we also may live new lives" (Romans 6:4, NLT).

The process of sanctification is the step-by-step process of surrendering ourselves to God and allowing God to change us to be more like Christ Jesus. When we do, we take one more step in walking in the light of God's salvation. Ask yourself these questions: Am I willing to believe what God's Word says about me and that the gifts He has for me are true for me today? Am I willing to allow Christ Jesus to fulfill in me the promises God has for me? Am I willing to allow God to finish the good work He has started in me so His plans for my good and the work He has for me to do will be accomplished in my life? I am often reminded of that old saying I grew up hearing: "Where there is a will, there is a way." The question is, however, are we willing to do it God's way?

Time of Reflection

For if the willingness is there, the gift is acceptable
according to what one has, not according to what one does
not have.

2 Corinthians 8:12 (NIV)

Describe the time when you realized God wanted you
to achieve more than you could achieve on your own. Were
you willing to believe in the dream He put in your heart?
Why or why not?

Does knowing God loves you unconditionally help you
accept and receive His best for you?

List three areas of your life in which God has been
prompting you to release what is weighing you down.

Take a few moments to pray and ask God to show you
any area in your life you have been unwilling to accept His
best or His Word in your life. Ask Him to give you the willingness and determination to do so.

Chapter 3

Heart to Receive

*The heart is deceitful above all things And it is extremely
sick; Who can understand it fully
and know its secret motives?*

Jeremiah 17:9 (AMP)

The word "heart" is mentioned over one thousand times in the Bible, meaning it bears much significance in a person's life. God says man looks at the outward appearance, but God looks at a person's heart (1 Samuel 16:7). What does God say about the heart?

Our heart is the spiritual part of us where we find our thoughts, intentions, and desires. We can say we know what is in our hearts, but do we? We are told God knows our hearts. He knows the secrets of every heart (Psalm 44:21).

God tests us to know what is in our heart (Deuteronomy 8:2). Therefore, it is important we do not make decisions based on our emotions because our emotions can change every day based on what we experience. What may seem right one day can show itself to be wrong the next. We should make decisions based on the truth of God's Word. "Who are those who fear the Lord? He will show them the path they should choose" (Psalm 25:12, NLT). "Delight yourself in the Lord, and he will give you the desires of your heart" (Psalm 37:4, ESV). There is a direct correlation between receiving the desires of our hearts and doing what God's Word says. What does it mean to have a heart to receive?

Unconfessed Sin

When we become Christians, we are a new creation. The Lord tells us,

> And I will give them one heart [a new heart], and put a new spirit within them. I will take from them the heart of stone, and will give them a heart of flesh [that is responsive to My

touch], that they may walk in My statutes and keep My ordinances and do them. Then they shall be My people, and I will be their God.

Ezekiel 11:19–20 (AMP)

With Jesus and the Holy Spirit within us, we can delight ourselves in the Lord and reject every kind of evil (1 Thessalonians 5:22). How do we do this? Work out your salvation with fear and trembling (Philippians 2:12).

Salvation should not be viewed as a one-time experience, and then we are set for life. We are on a journey to become more like Christ, and in doing so, we will overcome the struggles we face that work to keep us from maintaining a strong relationship with God. We are in a struggle with our own selfish desires, called our flesh. The world we live in offers many opportunities to feed the selfish desires of our flesh. Even as Christians, we are still required to confess our sins to the Lord and seek His forgiveness when we make mistakes. We can get so caught up in the busyness of living we do not realize we made a mistake, or we simply choose to overlook it. Either way, not confessing our mistakes to God on a regular basis will make us insensitive to the Holy Spirit when He guides us to make the right choices. Before you know it, everything seems to snowball out of control; we've lost our peace, and we can't figure out what went wrong.

It starts out small, like eating a few bites of crème brûlée. Rich and delicious! But you cannot stand the thought of the rest of this delicious dessert being thrown in the trash, so you have to finish it. Now you have gone to taste bud-heaven. Glorious! You got caught up in the moment and simply forgot that the Lord and your doctor have spoken to you many times about avoiding excessive sugar intake because of how it affects your health. Now you are not feeling so well. You once again realize for others something of this nature is fine, no problem, but not for you. You now have sin needing to be confessed to the Lord.

If you have ever seen a clogged sink, you notice the water builds up in the sink basin instead of readily draining as the water is flowing out of the faucet. The water takes a few minutes to drain. If the clogged drain is not cleaned, the water will continue to drain slowly, and eventually, the water will stand in the sink and become stagnant. The cost of taking the time to purchase a bottle of drain cleaner when the sink first began to drain slowly would have been relatively low. Because this was not done, now a plumber is needed to clean the clog and the cost will be greater.

Just like the sink, our hearts can become like clogged pipes. Confessing sin regularly is like using drain cleaner. Confessing sin on a regular basis will keep our hearts clean before God. When we do not, our hearts run the risk of becoming callous, causing us to be insensitive to God's voice when He speaks to our hearts. "The high and lofty one who lives in eternity, the Holy One, says this: 'I live in the high and holy place with those whose spirits are contrite and humble. I restore the crushed spirit of the humble and revive the courage of those with repentant hearts'" (Isaiah 57:15, NLT).

God is not oblivious to the challenges we face. Confession of sin does not require a processional of grief and tears for us to receive forgiveness, but God does require that we are sincere in our willingness to change and correct our behavior. God knows what is in our hearts.

Unforgiveness

Understanding forgiveness was difficult for me. I grew up in a solid Christian home, but I did not discover the need to forgive on a conscious level until after I became an adult and experienced more than I would ever be able to overlook during the course of an abusive marriage. My pastor told me, "You are going to have to forgive him. As long as you stay mad at him, he is controlling you." This set me free. When I finally left the abuse, I purposed in my heart to allow only God to be in control of me. With this release, not only did my emotions become more level, I experienced a peace I never before knew was possible.

The Lord tells us, "If you forgive those who sin against you, your heavenly Father will forgive you" (Matthew 6:14, NLT). Why is this important? Matthew 18:21–35 gives a good account of a king who wanted to settle his accounts of money that others owed him. One man owed him millions of dollars he could not pay. So the king ordered that he, his family, and all they had be sold. This man begged for forgiveness, and the king released him and forgave his debt. This same man, in turn, went to another man who owed him a few thousand dollars. This man told him he did not have the money to pay him back but asked him to give him some time, and he would pay back every penny. The man who was previously forgiven refused and had this man put in jail. A servant of the king heard about what had happened and told the king. The king called this man to him and said, "You evil servant! I forgave you that tremendous debt because you pleaded with me. Shouldn't you have mercy on your fellow servant, just as I had mercy on you?" (Matthew 18:32–33, NLT). Then, the angry king sent the man to prison until he had paid every penny. Where much is given, much is required (Luke 12:48).

Forgiving others can be difficult. Asking for forgiveness from others we have offended or hurt can likewise be difficult. "So if you are presenting a sacrifice at the altar in the Temple and you suddenly remember that someone has something against you, leave your sacrifice there at the altar. Go and be reconciled to that person. Then come and offer your sacrifice to God" (Matthew 5:23–24, NLT).

God paid a great price for our salvation. God gave us His best. When we do not forgive others after being forgiven of much, pride rises, which will cause us to stumble. Asking for forgiveness from someone does not always mean they will give it to you. Asking someone to forgive us for something we have done forces us to look at ourselves in the reality of who we are—someone in need of a Savior.

"Make every effort to live in peace with everyone and to be holy; without holiness no one will see the Lord. See to it that no one falls short of the grace of God and that no bitter root grows up to cause trouble and defile many" (Hebrews 12:14–15, NIV). God holds us to His standard of what is right. If unforgiveness is not properly dealt with, the heart will become dull and hard from the hurt and resentment, and a root of bitterness will develop. Before you know it, thoughts and conversations are consumed by the offense, and every relationship is affected by your experience (causing trouble and defiling many). Unforgiveness will even affect the choices we make. Staying focused on a wrong someone has done will eventually change the color of the lens you see others through, thus coloring every mistake with a tint of unforgiveness. Before long, you will become disgruntled, negative, and someone with whom others will have difficulty being around. Forgiveness does not mean we excuse the wrong done; it simply means we no longer allow ourselves to be controlled by or make decisions based on the hurt.

Selfish Desires

This seems simple enough to understand. We all want what we want. We have a need that must be fulfilled. We see something, we like it, we want it. It is done. Is it okay to desire great things? Does desiring great things not keep the Lord first in our lives? After all, God tells us if we delight ourselves in Him, He will give us the desires of our hearts.

The Lord tells us to "do nothing out of selfish ambition or vain conceit. Rather, in humility value others above yourselves, not looking to your own interests but each of you to the interests of the others" (Philippians 2:3–4, NIV). The very nature of God is that of a giving, compassionate heart—for God loved us so much He gave us His Son (John

3:16). Being selfish reflects following the desires of your sinful nature (Galatians 5:19). This leads to disorder and every kind of evil (James 3:16). Selfish desires are the root causes of why mankind was separated from God to begin with—the reason we need a Savior.

Jesus is our perfect example, and His very nature is to serve and not to be served. Matthew 20:20 tells us of two brothers, James and John, who wanted to sit in the places of honor next to Jesus in the kingdom of heaven. They gave little thought to how this would affect the other disciples. This, in turn, caused the other disciples to become angry and offended. Jesus told them that this selfish desire was being worldly-minded. Matthew 20:26–27 goes on to state that whoever wants to be first must become a servant. "For even I, the Messiah, am not here to be served, but to help others, and to give my life as a ransom for many" (Mark 10:45, TLB). Pride will cause us to consider only our interests and will usually cause strife with others along the way. Pride also sets us against God—just like Satan wanted to set his throne above the highest heavens and make himself like God (Isaiah 14:12–15). This pride got

Satan kicked out of heaven. When we allow pride to come into our hearts, we will soon fall further away from God (Proverbs 16:18). Jesus set the perfect example for us. Before we can lead, we must learn to follow.

A selfish heart will tear down and undermine relationships and friendships and destroy lives. Pride makes no consideration for God and others. If we are not careful, this pride will cause us to lose the humble attitude we have that allows God to give us His wisdom. God opposes the proud but gives grace to those with a humble heart (James 4:6).

God is concerned about all things concerning us. He wants us to have good things. He wants us to desire the good of this land. He wants us to enjoy the good of this land for ourselves. In all our giving to others, it is okay to give to yourself. God does not want the desire to give to ourselves to become what consumes us. God promises us in Jeremiah 29:13 that we will find Him when we seek Him with our whole heart—when nothing else is more important to us than Him.

We are told in James 4:2–3 (TLB),

> You want what you don't have, so you kill to
> get it. You long for what others have, and can't
> afford it, so you start a fight to take it away
> from them. And yet the reason you don't have
> what you want is that you don't ask God for
> it. And even when you do ask you don't get it
> because your whole aim is wrong—you want
> only what will give *you* pleasure.

"The blessing of the Lord makes a person rich, and he adds no sorrow with it" (Proverbs 10:22, NLT). God knows what we need and what we want. He asks us to trust Him for it.

Anything we want more than God, anything we rely on more than God, anything we look to for fulfillment rather than God, is an idol. It is the hidden sin driving all other sins.

> You shall not make for yourself any idol, or
> any likeness (form, manifestation) of what
> is in heaven above or on the earth beneath
> or in the water under the earth [as an object
> to worship]. You shall not worship them nor
> serve them; for I, the Lord your God, am a

jealous (impassioned) God [demanding what
is rightfully and uniquely mine].

Exodus 20:4–5 (AMP)

The very essence of our salvation stems from our
knowledge and recognition of our need for God in our lives
and our willingness to humble ourselves before Him to receive His goodness. "Guard your heart above all else, for it
determines the course of your life" (Proverbs 4:23, NLT).

Humility and Grace

While in church one Sunday night, I heard a story of a
man who was married to his wife for over fifty years. They
met when they were young, both from strong Christian
families. He was fortunate to have worked for the same
great company for thirty years, so he had an above-average
income and retired with a good pension. Their children
grew up and succeeded in their chosen fields. They had
families of their own who loved and served the Lord.
"Yes," he said, "It's because of God's grace we have

received such blessings in our lives with few difficulties along the way." God's grace is sufficient (2 Corinthians 12:9).

Then I heard the story of another man whose story was quite different. He was raised in a home where his father left soon after he was born. His mother worked hard to raise him, but he soon found himself searching for more than she could give and became involved in a gang. Shortly after, he began selling drugs. His life changed when he found the woman of his dreams and got married, thinking life had finally dealt him a good hand. They had two children. He tried to work and support his family, but the pressure became too much. He found himself being pulled back into the world he knew all too well, and a lifestyle of gang activity and drugs took over. His wife could no longer handle the lies and abuse, so she left with the kids and filed for divorce. The pain of losing his family spiraled him into a pit he could not climb out of, and he sought to end his life. A man walked up to him one day and shared the gospel of Jesus Christ with him. He gave his life to Christ. He was radically saved, and he walked away from the drugs and the life of crime. In time, he and his wife reconciled their relationship, and his marriage and family were restored. Soon thereafter, this man surrendered to the call of God on his life, and he became a youth pastor. "Yes," this man said, "It was because of God's grace I was delivered from drugs and life on the streets, got my family back, and now serve the Lord." God's grace is sufficient.

Grace. Getting something good we do not deserve. "The sacrifice you desire is a broken spirit. You will not reject a broken and repentant heart, O God" (Psalm 51:17, NLT). God seeks a heart that is humble and a heart that longs after Him.

Time of Reflection

Above all else, guard your heart, for everything you do

flows from it.

Proverbs 4:23 (NIV)

We discussed how unconfessed sin and unforgiveness can make our hearts become like a clogged sink. Discuss your thoughts.

Before this study, did you realize the importance of confessing sin to God and forgiving others? In what way?

Describe a time you held unforgiveness or unconfessed sin. How did this affect your life and your relationships?

Take the time to pray and ask God to search your heart and show you anything that hinders a closer walk with Him. Ask God to cleanse your heart and show you how to guard your heart.

Chapter 4

Perfect Love—Strength to Stand

And over all these virtues put on love, which binds them all together in perfect unity.

Colossians 3:14 (NIV)

What is Love?

There are many types of love. There is love found in a friendship, one of loving yourself, love for a spouse, and love for everyone, which is called agape love. Love is often represented with a heart on Valentine's Day or candy placed in a heart-shaped box or a card with warm-felt sentiments. Warm feelings surround us when family or friends gather to celebrate a new life or new-found success. Love is expressed through care and concern when we hear of tragedies, heartache, or loss.

First John 4:19 (NIV) tells us, "We love because he first loved us." God gives us the capacity to love and be loved because of His love. The question lingers, with this great love, why is there so much hate in this world? Think of love being a light bulb in a dark room. When the source of power (light switch) is turned on, the room is no longer dark. We are the light bulb in the darkness of this world. When we allow God to love us, the power source of His love causes the light of love within us to burn brightly and snuff out the darkness in this world.

God's Love for Us

For a long time, I didn't understand how a perfect God could love me so much that He would pursue me, rescue me, and save me. I later realized it was because His love for me does not depend on me. God is love.

The Bible explains it like this: "But God, being rich in mercy, because of the great love with which he loved us, even when we were dead in our trespasses, made us alive together with Christ—by grace you have been saved" (Ephesians 2:4–5, ESV). "In this is love, not that we have loved God but that he loved us and sent his Son to be the propitiation [the price that satisfied the payment required] for our sins" (1 John 4:10, ESV). Can you imagine someone loving you so much they would give their life for you? We can look to 1 Corinthians 13:4–8 to see what love is.

Love is patient. "The Lord is compassionate and merciful, slow to get angry and filled with unfailing love" (Psalm 103:8, NLT). He is good and ready to forgive and abundant in loving-kindness to all who call on Him. "The Lord is not slow in keeping his promise, as some understand slowness. Instead he is patient with you, not wanting anyone to perish, but everyone to come to repentance" (2 Peter 3:9, ESV). Love lets your child know it is okay when little hands spill flour as the help you make pancakes by not getting upset and simply saying, "It's okay. Just try again."

Love is kind.

> God our Savior revealed His kindness and love, he saved us, not because of the righteous things we had done, but because of his mercy. He washed away our sins, giving us a new

birth and new life through the Holy Spirit. He generously poured out the Spirit upon us through Jesus Christ our Savior. Because of his grace he made us right in his sight and gave us confidence that we will inherit eternal life.

Titus 3:4–7 (NLT)

Love gives a homeless person a meal, the shirt on your back, or the shoes on your feet to help supply their needs for one more day.

Love is not jealous. At first, this may seem contradictory, in that scripture in Exodus 34:14 (NLT) tells us we "must worship no other gods, for the Lord, whose very name is Jealous, is a God who is jealous about his relationship with you." The Hebrew word for "jealous" in this scripture is *qanna*, meaning "enthusiastic in His love for His children." In this context, the word "jealous" describes God's great love and passion for His children and His desire to give us His best. After I prayed for a wayward child to come home, I heard the Lord say, "I am jealous for her." He let me know His love for her was so great He would pursue her and not allow her to be taken from Him. "No eye has seen, nor ear heard, nor the heart of man imagined, what God has prepared for those who love him" (1 Corinthians 2:9, ESV). He knows the good He has for us, and He does not want us to miss out by turning away from Him.

To think of God as being jealous in the context of a humanistic view is to reduce God to being no different than a jealous husband who is jealous of the interactions his wife has with others. God is the One who created us and loved us into a relationship with Him. He does not want to take a back seat in our lives. He has done all He has done for us so we would not be separated from Him for eternity. After raising a child, loving them, providing for them, guiding them, and helping them obtain a good future, would you not be a little upset if the child credited someone else for the hard work you invested in them and the good they have obtained? Would you not be a little jealous if they gave all their time and attention to someone or something else while sharing the fruits of their good with others and ignored you? Yes, I believe so. We are made in God's image, in His likeness with like attributes. A big difference between us, however, is God has much more patience than we have. God is not a supernatural entity that sits in heaven waiting to strike us down for everything we do wrong. That is because God is love, and all He does for us stems from His love for us. Psalm 68:5–6 (NLT) says, "A father to the fatherless, a defender of widows, is God in his holy dwelling." All throughout the Bible, we read that God wants to be in a relationship with us. "Behold, I stand at the door and knock. If anyone hears my voice and opens the door, I will come in to him and eat with him, and he with me" (Revelation 3:20, ESV).

We understand being jealous as resentment toward a person for having or enjoying what we think should be ours. As described in 1 Corinthians 13:4, love is not envious of what a person has or enjoys. Every good and perfect gift is from God. God says He does not withhold good from those whose walk is right. "Riches and honor come from you alone, and you are the ruler of all mankind; your hand controls power and might, and it is at your discretion that men are made great and given strength" (1 Chronicles

29:12, TLB). God does not show favoritism. Instead of being envious of what someone has, ask God for what you desire to have. Tell the green-eyed monster to go and leave you alone.

Love does not brag. God gives each of us gifts and talents to fulfill His purpose in our lives. God gives us the ability to develop those talents. It is up to us to put forth the effort to develop those talents. Some put forth much effort, others very little. Receiving accolades for our talents is a gift from God. Remaining humble before God shows acknowledgment that our gifts, talents, and abilities are from Him. Give credit where credit is due. "For everything comes from him and exists by his power and is intended for his glory. All glory to him forever! Amen" (Romans 11:36, NLT). "So don't boast about following a particular human leader. For everything belongs to you" (1 Corinthians 3:21, NLT).

Love is not proud. Pride is when someone thinks nothing is more important than themselves or what they are trying to achieve, which is the opposite of what God says. God tells us it is better to give than to receive, and when we do, with great pleasure, God will give back to us much more than we give. Proverbs 6:16–19 states there are seven things God hates, one of which is haughty eyes. "Haughty eyes, a proud heart, and evil actions are all sin" (Proverbs 21:4, NLT). God gives grace to the humble, but He resists the proud. Great is the reward of those who are humble before God.

Love does not demand its own way. At one time or another, everyone has encountered that person who says, "It's my way or the highway" or "It's all about me." Love does not bully someone. Love does not desire to control someone through scare tactics and intimidation. Love does not demand dinner to be hot and on the table no matter what time that person comes home. Love encourages and allows us all room to grow. "Today I have given you the choice between life and death, between blessings and curses. Now I call on heaven and earth to witness the choice you make. Oh, that you would choose life, so that you and your descendants might live!" (Deuteronomy 30:19, NLT). God gives us a choice. Choose to let go and let God have control.

Love is not easily angered. Do you have thin skin or thick skin? We teach our children to stop, think, stay calm, and do not overreact. Most people have seen the destruction of life or property that comes from being easily angered. Love is patient when differences arise. Love covers a multitude of sins (1 Peter 4:8) just as God does for us. God is slow to anger because of His steadfast love for us (Psalm 103:8). Because of His great love for us, God delays His judgment so people would be saved (2 Peter 3:13). Our perfect example is Jesus. He lived a life experiencing many agitating factors thrown at Him. Yet, Christ Jesus never sinned. Take a deep breath before you act or speak. Keep your heart as soft as velvet and your skin as tough as leather, and know offenses are offered at a dime a dozen, so do not take them. Keep that loving smile on your face and direct your anger against the wrong, not against the person.

Love keeps no record of wrongs. As a youth, three of my friends and I acted in skits we wrote for our church, much like the following:

Every week, Opinions of the Saints records

were kept. On one particular occasion, the nursery worker's opinion was left out of the count. When news of this surfaced, Ms. Chatterbox could not contain herself, so a disclosure of the injustice was shared with Ms. Goodytwoshoes, who felt this could not be overlooked and, with stout eagerness, discussed the matter with Ms. Grumpypants, who, without hesitation and with feelings of reproach made known loudly and sternly, enlisted Ms. Minnie, the dear, sweet, cannot keep her opinion to herself with restraint saint whilst walking cane aimed, in turn, called for a special committee to look into the matter and give a full account of the Records of Wrong that had been kept for so long and report it before the entire church body. The church took sides, half for and half against the inclusion of said nursery worker's opinion into the count of the registry. Poor, poor nursery worker. Ms. Minnie cast the deciding vote. You should be present in church for your opinion to matter.

Let us love with the love of Christ. Love covers a multitude of sins. When "we confess our sins, he is faithful and just and will forgive us our sins and purify us from all unrighteousness" (1 John 1:9, NIV). He has removed our sins as far as the east is from the west (Psalm 103:12). Once we are forgiven, God does not keep a record of wrongs, and to Him, our opinion always matters.

"Love does not delight in evil but rejoices with the truth" (1 Corinthians 13:6, NIV). God tells us we are blessed and favored by Him when we do not act in the way of those who do evil. It is common for us to rejoice when a person who commits a crime is caught and put in jail for the evil act committed. But God says we should rejoice in truth. In this case, rejoice that evil can no longer continue to harm and delight in the hope that truth will be found and maintained. "I have no greater joy than to hear that my children are walking in the truth" (3 John 4, NLT). Jesus is the way, the truth, and the life, and no one comes to God except through Jesus (John 14:6). God's angels rejoice when a sinner repents and is saved (Luke 15:10). God's truth makes us free.

Love always protects. We do our best to protect our children from harm because we love them. God's love for us covers us with favor like a shield. He is our defender. He protects us from evil and will show the false allegations and lies that arise against our character to be wrong. "God

is our refuge and strength, a very present help in trouble"
(Psalm 46:1, ESV). He keeps His angels around us to
guard us and protect us in all our ways (Psalm 91). I had a
dream of someone I knew being harmed by her husband.
In the dream, she was driving frantically through a maze,
sometimes through heavily populated areas, trying to get to
a safe place. In the dream, she finally came to where I was
located and told me what was happening. In the dream, I
was able to help her find safety. When I woke up from the
dream, I knew this person was in danger and began to pray.
Ten years later, I asked her about what was happening in
her marriage during that time. She said her husband took a
fistful of her hair and dragged her across their front yard, as
one example. Soon after, she and her children were able to
leave that marriage, finding safety and peace. Even when
you may not see the evidence, God is always watching
over us to protect us and cause us to triumph. He works all
things together for our good (Romans 8:28).

Love always trusts. Love that trusts always has faith to
believe in you. It has confidence in you. Love never stops
believing in God and each other. "Through the power of

the Holy Spirit who lives within us, carefully guard the precious truth that has been entrusted to you" (2 Timothy 1:14, NLT). When we are in a relationship with someone, we trust our well-being to them. We trust they will keep confident our deepest secrets. We trust they will tell us truthfully their opinion about a life-changing decision we are facing when we ask them and not tell us something that they know will only cause us grief. God trusts that we will care for what He gives us, even after we make mistakes. Trust that God will always be with you, even when you cannot see His hand working in your situation. Trust that God will always see you through every situation.

Love always hopes. Hope is having full confidence in salvation and God's forgiveness. Hope also sees the potential of others. Hope always believes in a better tomorrow. Hope believes their hard work will accomplish something good in their lives. Jesus is our hope. His love is our lifeline to salvation. He knows the plans He has for us, plans for good and not harm, plans for a future with hope (Jeremiah 29:11). "Being confident of this, that he who be-gan a good work in you will carry it on to completion until the day of Christ Jesus" (Philippians 1:6, NIV). The oppo-site of hope is despair. Hope keeps the heart strong.

Love never fails. Love that never fails is not based on whims, feelings, trends, or based on what someone can do for you. Love that never fails is aimed at loving the seemingly unlovable. This kind of love does not retaliate after someone, who may not even know you, spreads despicable lies about you. This is the kind of love God shows us through every mistake we make. "Give thanks to the Lord, for he is good! *His faithful love endures forever.* Give thanks to the God of gods. *His faithful love endures forever.* Give thanks to the Lord of lords. *His faithful love endures forever*" (Psalm 136:1–3, NLT).

God's love for us is expressed in many ways. "And here is how to measure it—the greatest love is shown when a person lays down his life for his friends" (John 15:13, TLB).

God's Love in Us

"I have loved you, O my people, with an everlasting love; with loving-kindness I have drawn you to me"

(Jeremiah 31:3, TLB). God's love saves our souls and gives us new life. God's love in us becomes apparent in how we behave, in what we say, and in how we live. Understanding others will know God's love by how we live should encourage us to allow God to do His complete work in us. "You are the light of the world. A city set on a hill cannot be hidden" (Matthew 5:14, ESV). The light comes from Jesus, who is the light of the world (John 8:12). God's love in us causes us to be a light by which all men are drawn to Him.

One of the names of God is Jehovah Nissi—The Lord is our Banner. Exodus 17:6–19 describes a battle fought between the children of Israel and Amalek, one of their enemies. They won the battle against Amalek because God fought this battle through them. When an army advances, they lift up a banner showing who they are as they advance through territory. Imagine yourself being covered with a blanket from the top of your head to the bottom of your feet. When we are wrapped in a blanket, we are wrapped with a covering that protects us from cold. Like this blanket, God's love covers us completely and seals us with

His banner of love (book of Song of Solomon). His banner of love serves to show the territory you are advancing through that you belong to God, and God is saying, "This is My child. Get out of the way because they are coming through!" While we are advancing, Jesus is advancing before us and clears the way for us, making us more than conquerors. As Jesus covers us in His righteousness, He goes before us and makes way for us to succeed. God is for us, not against us. He crowns us with success, and wherever we place our feet, God gives us the land to possess. Do not be afraid!

Jesus is our banner through our daily advancements, giving us the strength to carry on, the courage to face fears, and the determination to try again after failed attempts. His love is a banner that causes us to triumph and prosper. His love is not given to us based on us being good enough to deserve it. His love is given to us in the totality of His capacity to give. His banner goes before us and announces to the presence of hindrances that we are children of God, and we will not be defeated. His love in us lets us know we belong to Him. His love in us tears down the walls within us, serving to keep us bound in doubt, defeat, and fear of rejection.

"There is no fear in love. But perfect love drives out fear" (1 John 4:18, NIV). Too many times, when God leads us to do something that will take us from where we are to where He wants us to be, we allow fear to creep in, which renders us unable to follow through. When we stand firm in God's love, fear is rendered powerless. We gain great confidence knowing God's love gives us strength. There are many who think that God is distant and uninvolved and that a personal relationship with Him is unattainable. God went to great lengths to prove His love for us in that while we were still sinners, God sent His Son, Jesus Christ, who died for us. His love is so great He pursues us by the power of His Holy Spirit, who opens our eyes to the need for a Savior and gives us faith enough to believe in Him.

Without God's love, we can do nothing good. With God's love, we can do all things through Christ, who gives us strength. The Lord watches over those who fear Him, those who rely on His unfailing love (Psalm 33:18, 20). Love is a basic human need. We all need to be loved. God's love in us causes us to overcome defeat and fulfill His purpose through us. His love in us perfects us to be more like Christ and able to stand in the presence of God.

God's Love Through Us

Allowing God to love us will transform our lives. His love for us not only forgives us, but it also has the power to heal us and change us from within so that our earthly vessels can allow God's love to be seen through us. As we are transformed into the likeness of Christ, we have a greater capacity to show God's love through us.

I heard a story of a woman who was married to a man who was bitter and harsh even in his dealings with her. He demanded that she care for not only his needs but also those of their home and the upkeep of their yard. Her friends, seeing her work tirelessly, encouraged her but found themselves at a loss for how to help her. She was not happy. She had no joy and no peace, which was apparent to all, but she was steadfast in her commitment to him, so she continued to do what he required of her. After some time, her husband died. She later married again, and her neighbors noticed her once again working tirelessly to meet the needs of her husband and her home, and yet again, she was even seen working in the yard. Exacerbated by this woman's behavior, they approached her to see why she continued in this manner. She admitted that before, her husband was not kind, and he was demanding in every way. But her new husband loved her and made no demands of her. She was pleased to do all this work to help him because he loved her unconditionally. He loved her into doing this. God's love for us is the same. He loves us without limit and without prerequisites. As we allow God to love us, our desire grows to want to serve Him wholeheartedly.

God's love is steadfast and sure. God's motivation to give us what is good is because He loves us. When you love someone, you are pleased to do good for them. Keeping God's commandments shows our love for God. "For the [true] love of God is this: that we *habitually* keep His commandments and remain focused on His precepts. And His commandments *and* His precepts are not difficult [to obey]" (1 John 5:3, AMP). God wants us "to know this love that surpasses knowledge—that you may be filled to the measure of all the fullness of God" (Ephesians 3:19, NIV). In this scripture, the words "to know" mean "to be made complete." Oh, that the whole world would know His love and be made complete in Him.

God tells us to love our neighbors as ourselves. At least once in your life, you have encountered one person who has tried your patience. Loving this neighbor without allowing your good nature to be tested beyond restraint can be accomplished when we allow the power of God's love to work through us. With God's help, we are able to share with our brothers and sisters who are in need (1 John 3:16–18), treat each other with kindness and patience (1 Corinthians 13:4), disciple the wayward sinner and restore with gentleness (Proverbs 3:11–12, Ephesians 6:1), and throw your arms around the prodigal son or daughter when they see their sin, come to their senses, and head for home (Luke 15:17–24). God often shows His love to us through other people. Being grateful enough to receive it shows our love and appreciation to Him.

Love is the strongest of all emotions, softening the harshness of anger, lessening fear, and stirring up hope.

Love is a steadfast commitment. As Christians, loving God is a steadfast commitment to loving Him and loving others. Studying God's Word teaches us how to love. Staying in communication with Him through our thoughts and prayer guides us in how to show love. "And so I am giving a new commandment to you now—love each other just as much as I love you. Your strong love for each other will prove to the world that you are my disciples" (John 13:34–35, TLB).

Loving others is a steadfast commitment to showing compassion without expecting them to accept it but always hoping they will. Do not be deceived; love does not abuse or spitefully use. Love does not demand its own way. Love protects and watches out for the welfare of others. Love does not say "Just get over it" and then walk away. Love takes the time to listen, even if you do not know what to say. Love does not condemn others for not understanding your needs.

At the end of the day, when you have loved all you can, and your storehouse of capacity to give is spent, go back to the source from where all love comes from and let Him love you to fullness again.

Love gives a smile to the heart of a lonely face.
Love always remains as you go on your way.
Love always, I give to you as I look into your face.
Love always, I give you with a warm embrace.
Love always. [4]

Time of Reflection

For I am convinced that neither death nor life, neither angels nor demons, neither the present nor the future, nor any powers, neither height nor depth, nor anything else in all creation, will be able to separate us from the love of God that is in Christ Jesus our Lord.

Romans 8:38–39 (NIV)

How does it make you feel to know God loves you unconditionally?

Do you struggle with believing God loves you unconditionally?

How does knowing God loves you, in spite of the worst things you have done, give you strength?

Take time to pray and ask God to show you His love for you. Ask God to reveal to you the ways He has shown you His love.

Chapter 5

Embrace the Cross—Faith to Believe

The message of the cross is foolishness to those who are

perishing, but to us who are being saved

it is the power of God.

1 Corinthians 1:18 (NIV)

Faith to Believe

The first step in knowing God is understanding the work of the cross. If a person does not understand the message of the cross, they will not understand to what great lengths God has extended His love for us. Understanding the reason for the cross of Calvary is vital in living a life of victory as a believer in Jesus Christ. God knew we would not be able to save ourselves. Before you and I were born, in His great love for all people, God paid the ransom to save us from our inherited sin nature with the precious lifeblood of Christ, the sinless, spotless Lamb of God, on the cross of Calvary. When we fully accept and receive the atoning work of the cross of Calvary, we will be set free.

The price for our sins was paid once and for all. When we accept Jesus as our Lord and Savior,

> We know that our old sinful selves were crucified with Christ so that sin might lose its power in our lives. We are no longer slaves to sin. For when we died with Christ we were set free from the power of sin. And since we died with Christ, we know we will also live with him. We are sure of this because Christ was raised from the dead, and he will never die again. Death no longer has any power over him. When he died, he died once to break the power of sin. But now that he lives, he lives for the glory of God. So you also should consider yourselves to be dead to the power of sin and alive to God through Christ Jesus.

Romans 6:6–11 (NLT)

The power of God that raised Jesus from the grave resides in us. This is the foundation of our faith. The cross is the power of God that works in us. This message alone will save the sinner, set the captive free, and cause us to live a life of victory in Christ Jesus.

Throughout our life experiences, "baggage" will develop, whether through relationships, work, hurts, disappointments, illness, loss, or many other life challenges. This baggage can result in walls we put up to protect our hearts from being damaged beyond repair. To fill the void our souls long for, too often, we look for escape by other means, whether through our own reasoning or the development of our own coping methods. This serves only as a bandage to cover a wound not even time can heal. God will take us out of our afflicted state and restore us on a strong foundation in Christ and make us exceedingly beautiful, pure, and stable, not despised or shamed. He will take the bad and turn it into good for our good. He will take the disappointments and reward faithfulness with success.

Isaiah 53 tells us what Jesus accomplished for us on the cross of Calvary. He bore our weaknesses and our sorrows.

He was wounded and crushed for our sins. He was beaten so that we would have peace. He was whipped, and by those stripes, we are healed. Jesus bore every sickness and disease on the cross of Calvary so that we could be healed. We have all strayed like sheep, leaving God's path to follow our own. The Lord laid on Jesus the guilt of sin for us. He was oppressed and treated harshly so that we would be set free from sin and death and walk in victory against the war waged against us in this world. We overcome by the blood of the Lamb and the word of our testimony (Revelation 12:11). Through the work on the cross of Calvary, we are more than conquerors because Jesus paid the price for our salvation, and we receive the great rewards.

Some may remember "The Bite Fight," a battle of brawn between heavyweight champion boxers Evander Holyfield and Mike Tyson. On June 28, 1997, a rematch was held between the two heavyweights after Holyfield beat out Tyson just seven months earlier for his third heavyweight championship title. In the third round, through engagement, Holyfield carelessly headed-butted Tyson and reopened a cut above his eye. Tyson, out of his frustration, bit off part of Holyfield's right ear and spit

it on the canvass in protest to Holyfield's head-butt. The

fight carried on for a short time, and if the first bite wasn't

enough, Tyson bit Holyfield again, this time on his left ear.

When the second bite was discovered, the fight ended with

Tyson being disqualified and Holyfield named the winner.

The outlandish behavior of Tyson made headline news

and was the talk of many around the world for years to

come. Holyfield is a Christian. When interviewed about his

championship and the incident with Tyson, Holyfield said

he already forgave Tyson for biting him and his complete

faith was in God and Jesus. As described by a local pastor,

Holyfield overcame this fight by his faith in God, his talent,

and his integrity. His church was more than a conqueror

when they accepted the tithe Holyfield gave on the $35

million salary he earned in that fight. As Christians, we

overcome by persevering in the race set before us and

not giving up when the fight gets hard. Jesus has already

fought and won the battle against sin and death on the

cross of Calvary. Like Holyfield's church, we are more

than conquerors when we accept the great reward salvation

brings through Jesus' sacrifice on the cross of Calvary by asking for forgiveness of our sins and asking Jesus to be Lord of our lives.

> In the same way God, in his desire to show to the heirs of the promise the unchangeable nature of his purpose, intervened *and* guaranteed it with an oath, so that by two unchangeable things [his promise and his oath] in which it is impossible for God to lie, we who have fled [to him] for refuge would have strong encouragement *and* indwelling strength to hold tightly to the hope set before us.

Hebrews 6:17–18 (AMP)

Through the cross of Calvary, we have the assurance of eternal salvation. Even amidst difficult times, life with God is always better than life without Him. The atoning work of the cross of Calvary is our only hope.

Are You Worth It?

In John 8:1–11, we read of Jesus visiting the Mount

of Olives. Early the next morning, He went back to the Temple. A crowd soon gathered, and he sat down and talked to them.

> As he was speaking, the Jewish leaders and Pharisees brought a woman caught in adultery and placed her out in front of the staring crowd. "Teacher," they said to Jesus, "this woman was caught in the very act of adultery. Moses' law says to kill her. What about it?" They were trying to trap him into saying something they could use against him, but Jesus stooped down and wrote in the dust with his finger. They kept demanding an answer, so he stood up again and said, "All right, hurl the stones at her until she dies. But only he who never sinned may throw the first!" Then he stooped down again and wrote some more in the dust. And the Jewish leaders slipped away one by one, beginning with the eldest, until only Jesus was left in front of the crowd with the woman. Then Jesus stood up again and said to her, "Where are your accusers? Didn't even one of them condemn you?" "No, sir," she said. And Jesus said, "Neither do I. Go and sin no more."

John 8:3–11 (TLB)

In this story, we find a woman who was almost killed without an opportunity for repentance. However, Jesus intercedes for her and points out to everyone that although what this woman did was an act of sin worthy of death, they, too, have also sinned. In their attempt to uphold the law, they did not hold themselves to the same standard of the law. As Jesus pointed out, this woman was not unworthy of forgiveness simply because of the "kind" of sin she committed. He pointed out to this woman that if He was willing to forgive her, she should be willing to accept it, even if others were not willing to acknowledge the possibility of forgiveness for her. This was a divine appointment for this woman. Jesus demonstrated His love for her by intervening for her. Many today will hold themselves apart from the law and condemn someone who makes even the slightest error. God does not measure or classify sin in this manner. Only man does this! God does not generalize or diminish sin. God judges sin on a finite level—sin is sin, and on the cross of Calvary, sin was atoned for once and for all, for all time, and all mankind willing to accept it.

What we deem unforgivable and what God deems unforgivable are too often miles apart. God says the only unforgivable sin is rejecting His Son, Jesus Christ, or blaspheming the Holy Spirit, who reveals the reality of who Christ Jesus is (Matthew 12:31–32). Finding peace and assurance of this can be overwhelming when facing the insurmountable odds of constant reminders of things gone wrong. Just as this woman had many accusers who were ready to stone her to death, we too have an accuser who wishes nothing more than we settle for defeat and be held captive in our regret. The true definition of repentance begins with sorrow for knowing you have done something wrong. Sadly, many people get stuck because they take on shame, not just remorse. They begin to wear the memories and feelings of guilt and regret like their clothes, thinking this is an effective form of penance. However, this only serves to foster planting the identity of shame, which takes root deeply and hinders the person's ability to accept forgiveness and move forward. Too many Christians find themselves bound in regret, and many remain stuck for years without ever understanding there is absolutely no reason for it.

To kill a weed in a garden, you must first kill the root. An experienced gardener will tell you choosing the proper weed killer is vital. An incorrect mixture can also kill the soil's ability to grow anything. On our journey, we must understand the garden of our soul where the hurts and regrets have been planted. If we choose to take on the blanket of shame and do not accept God's forgiveness and healing, our souls will soon become a garden full of weeds of despair and complacency. In doing so, we choke out the fruits the Holy Spirit of God has planted within us, thus hindering our ability to produce good fruit and prosper in the way God intended.

Jesus came to this earth to die on the cross of Calvary so that we would be set free. This shows how much God loves us. He knows Satan will attempt to keep wounds festering and even open old wounds to keep us from walking in the light of his salvation. There is power in knowing. Being firmly seated in knowing who we are in Christ and knowing God's love is unconditional is key. Even while Jesus was suffering the insufferable agony on the cross, He was still praying for us! Jesus did a complete work on the cross for all our needs. No one deserves God's love and goodness. Grace is a gift from God. God says we are worth it because He thinks we are. He simply asks us if we are willing to believe it, accept it, and receive it.

God Is Not Mocked

"Shall we keep on sinning so that God can keep on showing us more and more kindness and forgiveness? Of course not!" (Romans 6:1–2, TLB). If we have truly accepted Christ as our Savior, we are dead to sin. This means we no longer have the inward desire to wake up every day seeking our own pleasures with no regard for God's desires. "And if the Spirit of him who raised Jesus from the dead is living in you, he who raised Christ from the dead will also give life to your mortal bodies because of his Spirit who lives in you" (Romans 8:11, NIV). As a believer in Christ, the Holy Spirit's presence within us reveals sin. Even so, as God's children, we are still earthen vessels, and we must choose to walk away from the temptation of sin.

"Do not judge others, and you will not be judged. For you will be treated as you treat others. The standard you use in judging is the standard by which you will be judged" (Matthew 7:1–2, NLT). This does not mean we should excuse sin. No, we should call sin what it is—sin. God does. "Or do you not know that the Lord's people will judge the world?" (1 Corinthians 6:2, NIV). When we judge, we should not measure what someone does against what we do or how we think something should be done. Our paths are different, and we are all sinners in need of a Savior. We use God's truth to expose sin and then lead the person into truth with guidance from the Holy Spirit. Unfortunately, there will be people who do not want to hear God's message of hope. We are not responsible for someone else's salvation—that is the work of the Holy Spirit. We are simply God's messengers. We are responsible for living the change God made in us through Christ Jesus. God will not be mocked. He sees the hidden motives of the heart. "All a person's ways seem pure to them, but motives are weighed by the Lord" (Proverbs 16:2, NIV).

"Why worry about a speck in your friend's eye when

you have a log in your own? How can you think of saying to your friend, 'Let me help you get rid of that speck in your eye,' when you can't see past the log in your own eye?" (Matthew 7:3–4, NLT). In Psalm 139:23–24, King David asks God to search his heart, point out anything offensive to God, and lead him in the way that is good and everlasting. King David recognized his need to have a clean heart before God. As we discussed in chapter 3, having a clean heart before God keeps us sensitive to God's voice to know what He is saying and how we should share His truth with others. In doing so, we resist the temptation of self-righteousness, a sin of the flesh—a trap set by Satan to render our testimony tainted.

When we pray first, God is given the opportunity to prepare us and the hearts and minds of others to be receptive to what we will say. Be intolerant of sin but tolerant of the people who believe differently. There is freedom in knowing the work of salvation in others does not depend on us. We are simply the messengers God chooses to tell the world He loves them too. And by doing so, we store up treasures in heaven, where moth and rust will not destroy (Matthew 6:20).

There Is No Mistake Here

We can come to realize we are saved and then become complacent. When God saved us, He told us to make disciples of all nations. This means we share the testimony of what Jesus did for us and how our relationship with Jesus changed our lives.

> But how can they call on him to save them unless they believe in him? And how can they believe in him if they have never heard about him? And how can they hear about him unless someone tells them? And how will anyone go and tell them without being sent? That is why the Scriptures say, "How beautiful are the feet of messengers who bring good news!"
>
> Romans 10:14–15 (NLT)

When witnessing, it is important to understand how powerful our personal testimonies are. Everyone has a story. Every story is different. However, every testimony of our hope in Christ has the same thing in common: "I once was lost but now I'm found. I once was a sinner with no hope, but Jesus set me free" (John 8:36). People are watching you. They want to know if this "change" we are talking about is real.

Regardless of what anyone says, once God forgives us, He buries our sin as far as the east is from the west (Psalm 103:12). He will no longer hold it against us, and He will no longer hold us accountable for it. When we are reminded of our past for the purpose of stirring up sorrow and discontentment, this is the work of Satan, the accuser of the brethren. This world is full of lies and deceptions prepared to sell someone on the next big product that promises wholeness, happiness, healing, and fulfillment. People are looking for what is real. Christians need to live an authentic life in such a way that the light of Jesus and His love will shine through us. Jesus tells us that when He is lifted up, He will draw all men to Him (John 12:32).

There was a rich vineyard owner who went out early one day to find workers for his vineyard. He agreed to pay them a normal day's wages and sent them to work. He went out again at nine o'clock, then noon, at three o'clock, and then again at five o'clock, each time bringing in more workers to work. In the evening, he told the foreman to call the workers in and pay them, starting with those who were hired last and paid them a full day's pay. When those who were hired early in the day came in to get their pay, they assumed they would receive more, but they were paid the same amount of money as those who were hired at the end of the day. They became angry, thinking the owner was being unfair. Since they worked longer, they thought they should receive more pay. The rich vineyard owner answered and said, "I haven't been unfair! I kept my word to you. I paid you the normal day's wage you agreed to receive" (Matthew 20:1–16).

The rich vineyard worker is God. The wages are entry into heaven. The point is, it does not matter at what point you receive salvation through Christ; whether early in life or later, you get the same reward. We are saved by grace, through faith, not of works, so no man can boast (Ephesians 2:8). Every sin can be forgiven, except blasphemy of the Holy Spirit or outright rejection of Jesus Christ (Matthew

12:31). Blaspheming is the act of insulting or showing contempt or lack of reverence for God. The pitfall here is many people believe the misconception "I have plenty of time." No one knows the day or the hour Jesus will return or when their time on this earth will be over. Once your time on this earth is over, it is too late to change your mind and choose Christ. "Just as people are destined to die once, and after that to face judgment, so Christ was sacrificed once to take away the sins of many; and he will appear a second time, not to bear sin, but to bring salvation to those who are waiting for him" (Hebrews 9:27–28, NIV). Do not let it be said you waited one day too late.

People put measures, standards, levels, and categories on sin. God does not. Becoming a Christian does not make us perfect. Salvation through Jesus has given us freedom from sin. This freedom is not a license to do whatever we want to do. Instead, salvation gives us the ability to do what we should do. Being Christians means we have direct access to God, where we will find mercy and grace in our time of need. Being Christians does not mean we have all the answers to life; it means we can talk directly to the One who does. Jesus said, "I have told you all this so that you may have peace in me. Here on earth you will have many trials and sorrows. But take heart, because I have overcome the world" (John 16:33, NLT). There is no need to settle for the struggle. Embrace the cross and the victories it represents (Colossians 2:13–15).

Time of Reflection

May the God of hope fill you with all joy and peace as you

trust in him, so that you may overflow with hope by the

power of the Holy Spirit.

Romans 15:13 (NIV)

Where does your hope lie? What does the cross of Calvary mean to you?

Read Isaiah 53:4–5. List five things the atoning work of the cross of Calvary did for you.

Read Romans 8:11. What does this mean to you? Do you find hope in this promise?

Take the time to pray and thank God for Jesus and the finished work of the cross. Ask Him to show you how the cross has changed you.

Chapter 6

God Given Dominion—Take Authority

Jesus came and told his disciples, "I have been given all authority in heaven and on earth."

Matthew 28:18 (NLT)

Understanding Your Authority

Authority is the power or right to give orders, make decisions, and enforce obedience. As parents, we have authority over our children in that we have the right to say what they can and cannot do. As a business owner, one has authority over the employees who work in the business, and they have the authority to determine how the business is to be operated. Dominion is the authority or control over an area or territory.

In the garden of Eden, man gave up the authority God originally gave them. Authority on this earth, at that moment, was given to the prince of this world. However, when Christ was crucified, He redeemed us from the curse of sin and death. "Now is the time for judgment on this world; now the prince of this world will be driven out" (John 12:31, NIV). The prince of this world is the one who originated the plan of destruction against Adam and Eve, thus causing the original sin. The prince of this world is Satan, also called the devil, known as the enemy, and will be discussed in greater detail in chapter 7.

> I pray that your hearts will be flooded with light so that you can understand the confident hope he has given to those he called—his holy people who are his rich and glorious inheritance.
>
> I also pray that you will understand the incredible greatness of God's power for us who believe him. This is the same mighty power that raised Christ from the dead and seated him in the place of honor at God's right hand in the heavenly realms. Now he is

far above any ruler or authority or power or leader or anything else—not only in this world but also in the world to come. God has put all things under the authority of Christ and has made him head over all things for the benefit of the church. And the church is his body; it is made full and complete by Christ, who fills all things everywhere with himself.

Ephesians 1:18–23 (NLT)

Of What Authority Do You Speak?

But God is so rich in mercy, and he loved us so much, that even though we were dead because of our sins, he gave us life when he raised Christ from the dead. (It is only by God's grace that you have been saved!) For he raised us from the dead along with Christ and seated us with him in the heavenly realms because we are united with Christ Jesus. So God can point to us in all future ages as examples of the incredible wealth of his grace and kindness toward us, as shown in all he has done for us who are united with Christ Jesus.

God saved you by his grace when

you believed. And you can't take credit for this; it is a gift from God. Salvation is not a reward for the good things we have done, so none of us can boast about it. For we are God's masterpiece. He has created us anew in Christ Jesus, so we can do the good things he planned for us long ago.

Ephesians 2:4–10 (NLT)

We are made alive in Christ. We are no longer in sin and dead through Adam. We are seated in high places with Christ, meaning, in Christ, our works are made complete and acceptable. We are not saved by works but for works. Our works had nothing to do with our being saved. God's thoughts are higher than ours. Being seated with Christ means God already sees us in heaven with Christ. Even though we are not yet there—in God's eyes, we are.

When we become Christians, we are adopted into the family of God and become His sons and daughters. "God decided in advance to adopt us into his own family by bringing us to himself through Jesus Christ. This is what he wanted to do, and it gave him great pleasure" (Ephesians 1:5, NLT) in that "God sent him [Jesus Christ] to buy freedom for us who were slaves to the law, so that he could adopt us as his very own children" (Galatians. 4:5, NLT). God made us to have dominion over everything on this earth (Genesis 1:26–28). When we become Christians, we now have full rights as sons and daughters of the Lord God Almighty.

Through Christ Jesus, we are legally given authority by God to function in this world as His representatives, as ambassadors for Christ. Through the power of the Holy Spirit who resides in us, everything is available to us to partner with Him in life—favor, wisdom, knowledge, power, healing, and more—all of which is given to us when we accept Jesus as our personal Lord and Savior. It is of utmost importance that, as God's children, we understand who we are in Christ and the authority we are given. God did not abandon us to struggle through difficulties and setbacks. Being seated with Christ Jesus in high places means God has made us to share in His authority over His creation. This is not something that happens when we get to heaven.

We are seated there now. God destined His children to rule and reign in victory and have dominion and authority over everything on this earth. [5]

> Jesus came and told his disciples, "I have been given all authority in heaven and on earth. Therefore, go and make disciples of all the nations, baptizing them in the name of the Father and the Son and the Holy Spirit. Teach these new disciples to obey all the commands I have given you. And be sure of this: I am with you always, even to the end of the age."

> Matthew 28:18–20 (NLT)

We are given work to do. God has a plan and a purpose for us, and it is unique to each of us. We are to live our lives in such a way that no matter where we go, we will show how God has changed us and given us new life through His love and the power of the resurrection of Jesus Christ.

Simply being given this authority and saying we have

this authority is not going to produce godly results. We must come to understand the areas in our lives He has given us to influence and then commit to being a person who will work to bring about the changes God wants. Now would be a good time to ask yourself what God's plan and purpose is for your life. When you know this, determine what areas of influence God wants you to walk in the authority He has given you. In Christianity, you will hear it said there are seven mountains of influence in our society in which we are to influence for good. These are business, government, media, arts and entertainment, education, family, and religion. Some would argue Christians do not belong in these areas, but only in our personal lives and in a church. But further study of God's Word tells us we are to be a righteous influence everywhere we go and in whatever we do. Matthew 5:13–16 tells us that we are the salt of the earth, but that if the salt loses its flavor, it is useless. If we do not use the gifts and talents God has given us in every area of influence we have the opportunity, we are not walking in obedience to His Word.

Two of the scriptures that come to mind when I think

about being a good influence in our society is Deuteronomy 6:7, which says we are to teach God's Word to our children and talk about them when we wake up, when we lie down and when we go about our day. The other is found in Deuteronomy 28:1–14. God very plainly tells us He will bless us in every area of our lives if we will obey what He tells us to do. Deuteronomy 28:3 (NIV) tells us, "You will be blessed in the city and blessed in the country," and Deuteronomy 28:6 (NIV) tells us, "You will be blessed when you come in and blessed when you go out." In the city and in the field, when you come in and when you come out. I am a country girl at heart, so that tells me I am going to be blessed by God no matter where I go and no matter what I do. That is, as long as what I do and say is in obedience to God's Word and will. There are many areas to be influenced for good in the city. There are many areas to be influenced for good in the smaller communities as well. If we want to continue to live in peace in this world and our children and grandchildren to live in a peaceful world, we must take our rightful places of authority as given to us by God. "Have I not commanded you? Be strong and courageous. Do not be afraid; do not be discouraged, for the Lord your God will be with you wherever you go" (Joshua 1:9, NIV). "Look, I am giving all this land to you! Go in and occupy it, for it is the land the Lord swore to give to your ancestors Abraham, Isaac, and Jacob, and to all their descendants" (Deuteronomy 1:8, NLT). What land has God given you to occupy?[6]

Speak That Which Is Not as Though It Were

To begin, we must determine what God says is His final authority. When a child comes to their parent for permission to do something or get an explanation of a certain matter, the parent tells them what is permissible and what they expect from their child. The parents give their word on the matter. The same is true with God. The Bible is God's Word on a matter, and His Word is the final authority pertaining to all matters on this earth. We are given dominion and authority through Christ Jesus. We speak God's Word in Jesus' name, in His authority. There is power in the name of Jesus. There is no higher name than the name of Jesus, and all who call on the name of Jesus will be saved.

"I tell you the truth, whatever you forbid on earth will be forbidden in heaven, and whatever you permit on earth will be permitted in heaven" (Matthew 18:18, NLT). When we take authority, we speak what will be bound, so it is given no more power to work against a situation or a person. God backs up what you speak, and angels working with the Holy Spirit will be sent to cause the evil to be bound so it cannot continue to wreak havoc. When we speak God's acceptable solution into a situation, it is loosed or released into the heavenly realm to be accomplished, and God will then loose (release) the solution to come to pass. God tells us, "You may ask me for anything in my name, and I will do it" (John 14:14, NIV). In the beginning was the Word. He was with God, and He was God. He was in the beginning with God. He created everything there is. Nothing exists that He didn't make (John 1:1). Everything that has come into existence came into being by God's spoken word. We are given His authority to reign on this earth, and when we speak His Word in His authority, in Jesus' name, it goes forth and accomplishes everything

God sends it out to accomplish. "And the Lord said, 'That's right, and it means that I am watching, and I will certainly carry out all my plans'" (Jeremiah 1:12, NLT).

This does not mean we can speak whatever we want and expect it to be honored by God. When we speak God's acceptable solution, God will honor it. When we stand on the authority of God's Word, God will honor it. Speaking God's Word gives life to our lives and the world around us. "Those who love to talk will suffer the consequences. Men have died for saying the wrong thing!" (Proverbs 18:21, TLB) God will not be mocked. Whatever a man sows, he will reap (Galatians 6:7). Our words have power. We are held responsible for the words we speak. "But I tell you, on the day of judgment people will have to give an accounting for every careless or useless word they speak" (Matthew 12:36, AMP). Our words can heal, and our words can hurt. Carefully chosen, our words can bring about a God change that will produce life in souls and situations around the world. His Word is life to all our flesh. Therefore, speak life, speak God's Word. Speak words that will lift up, build up, and produce the good God wants.

God does not give us a spirit of fear but of power, love, and a sound mind (2 Timothy 1:7). It is interesting that the specific words God chose to state this are "spirit of fear." We have the authority to bind and cast out doubt, fear, or any opposing difficulty in our lives that hinders our relationship with God and hinders our fulfilling God's purpose and plan in our lives. We have the authority to tell them, "No! You can't stay here any longer! Leave!" We teach our children to "just say no" to things that will harm them. The same is true in our Christian walk. Tell the doubt to go. Tell the negative thinking to go. Say no to things that bring destruction. Tell yourself you can do all things through Christ, who will always cause you to triumph. The key is having faith and determination to do so by loosing God's will into our lives and those around us by speaking God's Word into situations. It is God's Word that brings change. It is God's anointed Word that releases us from the troubles bound to us. All the promises found in God's Word are "yes" and "amen" (2 Corinthians 1:20).

Although we cannot control what others do or say, we can make a difference in what we say and how we say it. In the beginning, God spoke to the vast expanse of void and spoke into existence the world as we know it—He spoke things into existence that were not there (Romans 4:17). Job 22:28 tells us whatever we decree shall be done. In praying for a friend, I found myself saying, "I bind the ill effects of careless words spoken, for no weapon formed against us will prosper, and any word spoken against us will be proven to be wrong." Speak God's Word to combat the fiery missiles of weapons formed against you, brush the dust off, and keep on going. We are given this same authority through salvation with Christ.

In Matthew 21:18–20, Jesus was hungry and went to a fig tree and found nothing on it. Jesus cursed the tree and said, "May no fruit ever come from you again!" (Matthew 21:19, ESV). The fig tree withered and died. We are given the authority through Christ to curse a situation or a sickness at its root, just as Jesus did to the fig tree. Then, we speak healing into the situation or person's body—we speak life according to God's will.

And Jesus answered them, "Have faith in

God. Truly, I say to you, whoever says to this mountain, 'Be taken up and thrown into the sea,' and does not doubt in his heart, but believes that what he says will come to pass, it will be done for him. Therefore I tell you, whatever you ask in prayer, believe that you have received it, and it will be yours."

Mark 11:22–24 (ESV)

We are in the position of authority to raise our children, and we are responsible for how we raise them. We are given the unique opportunity to speak life into them and their futures; for example, "You are loved," "You handled that situation well." We could also speak difficulties into them as well; for example, "You are stupid," "You will never amount to anything good." Be mindful that how we speak is as important as the words themselves. We speak volumes to our children and others through our verbal delivery and mannerisms. This mode of communication always seems to find its way back to us in one way or another. God promises us when we "train up a child in the way he should go; even when he is old he will not depart from it" (Proverbs 22:6, ESV). The Lord also tells us: "Don't keep on scolding and nagging your children, making them angry and resentful. Rather, bring them up with the loving discipline the Lord himself approves, with suggestions and godly advice" (Ephesians 6:4, TLB). "A gentle answer deflects anger, but harsh words make tempers flare" (Proverbs 15:1, NLT). "Set a guard, O Lord, over my mouth; Keep watch over the door of my lips [to keep me from speaking thoughtlessly]" (Psalm 141:3, AMP). What we say has power, so in all your getting, get knowledge and understanding (Proverbs 4:7). Speak life into others so the good seeds you sow in their lives will come back as a good harvest in your life. Do not get discouraged when the lessons need repeating. God rewards our efforts.

Before my son was born, I put Bible scripture on tape into a Walkman and put the headphones on my stomach. Every time my son heard the book of Psalms, it felt as if he was doing somersaults. Throughout the day, I spoke life-affirming words and good things to my son. My son was born autistic. My son was also born with an instinctive knowledge of the Word of God. I still speak life into my children and grandchildren today even though they cannot hear me say it: "My children and grandchildren will love and trust the Lord always (Proverbs 3:5, Luke 10:27); they will listen to and follow the voice of the Good Shepherd, and the voice of the stranger they will not follow (John 10:14, John 10:5); success and favor surround them like a shield (Psalm 5:12); they are sealed in righteousness, and they are sealed for greatness (Ephesians 1:13)." Encourage your children and teach them the way of the Lord. Encourage your children to do the same as they continue their own journey in life. If you do not, who will? Victory in this life is not achieved by good merits alone but by the Spirit of the Lord and His Word.

We can build people up instead of using our words carelessly, which only serves to tear people down. When we put our words in agreement with God and set our actions in agreement with God's Word, then we will see God work in our lives in accelerated motion like never before. [7]

Do Not Waver

> If you need wisdom, ask our generous God, and he will give it to you. He will not rebuke you for asking. But when you ask him, be sure that your faith is in God alone. Do not waver, for a person with divided loyalty is as unsettled as a wave of the sea that is blown and tossed by the wind.

James 1:5–6 (NLT)

"The Lord himself will fight for you. Just stay calm" (Exodus 14:14, NLT). Even though you may not see instant results, stand firm in your faith, knowing that God is in control and that His Word has the power to change your life and the world around you. Jesus releases the authority of His Word as it goes forth throughout the earth for the fulfillment of His purpose. We, as His representatives, are responsible for trusting His Word, living according to His Word, and speaking His Word to bring about His perfect will in our lives and in our world.

I love going to a quiet place in my yard to pray. One day, the Lord told me, "Take authority." It later occurred to me I was looking at a large, tall oak tree in my front yard. In many countries around the world, the oak tree symbolizes strength, endurance, success, and stability.

> Blessed are those who trust in the Lord and have made the Lord their hope and confidence. They are like trees planted along a riverbank, with roots that reach deep into the water. Such trees are not bothered by the heat or worried by long months of drought. Their leaves stay green, and they never stop producing fruit.
>
> Jeremiah 17:7–8 (NLT)

Our strength and confidence come through trusting God's faithfulness to keep His promises.

Understand the authority God gives you. Know the areas of influence God gives you and stand on His Word to accomplish His purpose. "Ask and it will be given to you; seek and you will find; knock and the door will be opened to you" (Matthew 7:7, NIV). Be willing to accept and receive the direction He has given you. Be willing to do all things as if you are doing them for the Lord Himself. Stand firm on His Word as the final authority in every area of your life. Continue to seek the Lord for what He is saying to you. In a relationship with God, you will never do life alone. Stand firm and steadfast as He continues to make you a strong, righteous oak for His glory (Isaiah 61:3).

Time of Reflection

Very truly I tell you, whoever believes in me will do the works I have been doing, and they will do even greater things than these, because I am going to the Father.

John 14:12 (NIV)

Describe what authority means to you. What kind of authority was adhered to in your home while you were growing up?

Are you willing to accept and use the authority God has given you?

What could keep you from standing in your authority as a Christian?

Take the time to pray and ask God to help you understand the extent of authority God has given you and the wisdom to know how to walk in that authority as His child.

Chapter 7

The Enemy Exposed

Our fight is not against people on earth. We are fighting
against the rulers and authorities and the powers of this
world's darkness. We are fighting against the spiritual
powers of evil in the heavenly places.

Ephesians 6:12 (ERV)

Becoming Christians means we are forgiven and
justified as righteous in God's eyes, meaning we are
cleansed white as snow as if we had never made a mistake.
Even so, it is not always easy to live as Christ says we
should live. Have you ever wondered why? Jesus said, "I
saw Satan falling from heaven as a flash of lightning! And I
have given you authority over all the power of the Enemy"
(Luke 10:18–19, TLB). I found myself asking, "What is

this enemy, Satan, that Jesus is talking about?" I was raised in church and became a Christian when I was nine years old, but it would take me many years to discover the truth about this enemy. While growing up, after seeing someone commit an indiscretion, I often heard "The devil made me do it" with a smile on their face, as if it were of no great significance. For many years, when I thought of the devil, I thought of what I had seen in old cartoons as a red devil on one shoulder and an angel on the other shoulder—the devil trying to convince you to do whatever you want and justifying why it is okay, and the angel warning you not to do it—the story of good versus evil. That was the only picture I had in my thoughts to guide my knowledge of him. As is usually the case, when things fell apart in my life, I began to ask the questions leading to the truth.

The term "Satan" is used many times in the Old Testament and the New Testament. The term "Satan" means "to oppose or be in opposition to"—an adversary. Some think of Satan as a legend or a myth. Then again, the fact that Satan does not like to be exposed before his evil work is done is one way he is found to be deceptive. We are first told about Satan in Genesis 3 when he tempted Eve to eat the apple, which she in turn offered to Adam, who in turn ate the apple, which brought sin to all mankind. Satan rose against Israel and caused David to take a census (1 Chronicles 21:1). God was displeased with the census David took, and as a result, God punished Israel. Reading further into 1 Chronicles 21 shows God's mercy to King David and Israel upon King David's obedience to God. Job 2:1–2 tells us of a conversation Satan had with God concerning Job, wherein Satan devises plans of attack against Job to test his faithfulness to God. Reading through Job, we find the very real struggle Job endured. Many times, we have intense struggles ourselves without understanding why. The purpose of this chapter is to reveal the root cause of many of these struggles.

In the New Testament, the term "Satan" refers to an adversary, opponent, or enemy. In Matthew 4:1–11 and Luke 4:1–13, we find Satan again when he came to Jesus in the wilderness and tempted Jesus to sin. In Luke 22:31, Jesus tells Peter that Satan has come to sift him like wheat. It stands to reason if so much emphasis is made on letting us know there is an enemy called Satan, we should take the time to understand who this enemy is and how he works against us.

Understanding the Enemy

"George Washington wrote in 1799, '…make them believe that offensive operations, often times, is the surest, if not the only (in some cases) means of defense.'"[8] In more contemporary terms and heard many times in sports arenas, it is stated, "The best defense is a good offense." For an army to defeat its enemy, they must learn who their enemy is. They observe them, studying their habits, their mannerisms, and their tactics. They must gain an understanding of their objective, which is to play against their enemy's weakness, and they will use any means available to accomplish this. When they understand how their enemy operates, they can wage a successful plan of attack against them.

We need to understand this about our enemy, who is Satan. Why is Satan against us? Because Satan wanted to be God, not serve God. Satan's pride got him kicked out of heaven, as stated in 1 John 3:8, Isaiah 14:12–14, and Ezekiel 28:12–18. Satan is against us because he is against God in us. In the garden, man gave Satan authority over the earth when he sinned against God. Understanding this is key to living a victorious life on this earth. We are not permanent residents of this earth. We are only passing through (Hebrews 13:14, TLB). As Christians, our eternal home is in heaven. We can make a difference in the eternal destiny of the souls on this earth with our testimony of salvation. In doing so, Satan and his methods of keeping people separated from God are rendered powerless. Satan knows we have the authority and ability to disarm him and advance the kingdom of heaven. Satan does not want us to operate it our authority because he knows his work will be defeated. Satan works against us through our hearts and minds to cunningly orchestrate his plan of attack against people and the church.

Satan is a liar, the father of lies, as stated in John 8:44. He is the original liar. For example, God told Adam and Eve not to eat of the fruit of the tree of the knowledge of good and evil because in doing so, they would surely die.

Satan tells them that they would not surely die, that their eyes would be open, and that they would be like God. This was a lie mixed with deception that fostered pride. God gives grace to the humble but resists the proud. So, if you hear a lie, even a simple white lie, the underlying root source is from the father of all lies.

Satan is the deceiver, "the one deceiving the whole world" (Revelation 12:9, NLT). Satan is very cunning, very sly. He has been at his game for a very long time. He has deceived people and nations into thinking that what is wrong is right and vice versa. He can make even the very thing God has told us to stay away from look right to us. Deception is conceived through lies. Satan is the father of lies, and there is no truth in him (John 8:44). Gaslighting is a form of deception. It is coercive control with the intent of brainwashing. We have seen this throughout our history books during the great wars. This is all too common in our world today through the information highway and social media.

Satan is the author of confusion. God is not the author of confusion, but the God of peace (1 Corinthians 14:33).

Have you ever experienced peace amidst confusion? All things are to be done in order (1 Corinthians 14:40). How do we know what is of God and truth and what is not? It must line up or come into agreement with God's Word. The Spirit of Truth (the Holy Spirit) who resides in us will confirm God's truth. Satan knows God's Word. He does not want the world or God's children to know and understand God's Word and the power within it because he knows God's truth sets us free. He has worked hard to separate and divide the church—the body of Christ—because "a home filled with strife and division destroys itself" (Mark 3:25, TLB). A destroyed home will not accomplish anything good, which is Satan's hope for mankind.

Satan is the one who comes to steal, kill, and destroy. "The thief's purpose is to steal, kill and destroy. My purpose is to give life in all its fullness" (John 10:10, TLB). Satan was a murderer from the beginning and has always hated the truth. There is no truth in him (John 8:44). Satan is here to cause dissention and strife. Therefore, God put much effort into telling us to guard our hearts. God tells us we know that we have passed from death to life because we love our brothers.

> If we love our brothers and sisters who are
> believers, it proves that we have passed from
> death to life. But a person who has no love is
> still dead. Anyone who hates another brother
> or sister is really a murderer at heart. And you
> know that murderers don't have eternal life
> within them.

1 John 3:14–15 (NLT)

Satan is the thief who comes to steal, kill, and destroy, and hate comes from him. Satan will take advantage of a difficult situation in a person's life and cause excessive, ongoing feelings of hate, bitterness, hopelessness, and helplessness by continuing to remind the person of losses and failures. This is one way he has convinced millions of people to give in to hopelessness and despair by giving up and taking their own lives or convincing others to give up on their hopes and dreams. Deception bred through lies is another way many are convinced that freedom of choice gives them the right to end the lives of unborn children.

Satan is the accuser of the brethren. "I heard a loud voice in heaven, saying, 'Now the salvation and the power and the kingdom of our God and the authority of His Christ have come, for the accuser of our brothers has been thrown down, who accuses them day and night before our God'" (Revelation 12:10, ESV). We are not perfect. We will make mistakes. Satan is also aware of the fact that when we confess our sins before the Father, we are forgiven. However, in his attempt to keep us from being strong in our relationship with Christ, he never misses an opportunity to remind us of our mistakes and misfortunes. He loves to rub salt into a wound. He will taunt and provoke the grief of defeat as long as we allow him. He will keep our minds and hearts swimming in regret if we let him. Do not give the devil a foothold. Stand up to him and immediately tell him you know who you are in Christ, and God does not measure your success by your mistakes. Remind him that he will spend eternity in the lake of fire while you will spend eternity in heaven with all the great saints of faith. Forgive those who have spoken against you, and pray for everyone to rise and walk in God's strength.[9]

Just as God is no respecter of persons, neither is Satan. Just as God has a plan for us for good and not harm, a future with hope, Satan has a plan against us—not to cause us to have a bad day but to destroy us. We are in a war, a daily battle between good and evil brought on by the evil one, Satan. "For we are not fighting against flesh-and-blood enemies, but against evil rulers and authorities of the unseen world, against mighty powers in this dark world, and against evil spirits in the heavenly places" (Ephesians 6:12, NLT) who are trying to destroy humanity through lies, deception, confusion, and any way they can to keep us from knowing and understanding God's truth and living the fullness of life through Christ.

Worthy of note is the story of Job. In Job 1:6–12, we read about a conversation between God and Satan. In this conversation, Satan is in the courtroom of heaven with God. In verses 9–11, Satan makes a case against Job, claiming that if God would allow him to bring catastrophe against Job, then Job would turn away from God and curse Him.[10]

Throughout this entire story, we find the struggles Job endures and the endless justifications given to Job by his well-meaning friends as the cause of these devastating curses. Even Job's wife cannot handle the struggle and advises Job to "curse God and die." Instead, Job, though he wanted to die so that his suffering would end, does not turn away from God. Instead, he gives a rightful place to God as the supreme and sovereign God He is. There is no explanation given or understanding found as to why the disaster and misfortune came upon Job and his family. Job's faith was tested. In the end, in the courtroom of heaven, Job was found to be as God said he was, blameless and favored by God. In turn, God restored to Job double of everything taken from him. In the courtroom of heaven, Satan was found to be the liar and thief he is. The war Satan waged against Job was defeated by God's sovereignty and His Word working in Job's life.

A lie that is too often accepted and believed is "If God is a loving God, why do bad things happen to good people?" Bad things happen because of sin in this world—not because God does not love us. If Satan can cause us to be blind to God's truth, which will save us, he has achieved his goal. If Satan can cause us to be deaf so that we do not hear the voice of the Lord that tells us He is here for us, he has achieved his goal. If Satan can cripple us so we cannot walk in the saving power of Christ, he has achieved his goal. The sooner we come to terms with this and get armed properly to fight effectively, the sooner we will walk in the light of God's salvation. Another lie is "If God is so good, why does He send people to hell?" The truth is, God does not send people to hell. God gives everyone a free will. He allows everyone a choice. Every day, we choose what we believe, what we say, what we do. If a person chooses not to believe or accept Jesus as God's way to spending eternity in heaven, they are ultimately choosing the opposite, which is spending eternity in hell, forever separated from God.

Satan is also the tempter, as stated in 1 Thessalonians 3:5. He uses any opportunity available to prevent the obedience of God's children. He entices us with our weaknesses—for example, the things we like because they taste good or make us feel good or feel good about ourselves—to set in motion a plan of destruction against us. God is omnipresent. Satan is not. Satan cannot be everywhere at the same time. However, he has his army of demons positioned to see and hear everything going on in what we call this natural world.

Satan and his demons do not know your thoughts. Satan is not omnipresent. Only God has this ability. First Kings 8:39 tells us only God knows our hearts. God is all-knowing. No one else has that ability. God even knows what we will say before we say it (Psalm 139:4). Satan, however, can see and hear everything we do and speak. He sees how we react and respond to situations, which gives him more insight into our current state of mind and emotions. In turn, this allows Satan to strike with another blow. "Be wise as serpents, and innocent as doves" (Matthew 10:16, AMP).

Proverbs 18:21 tells us the words we speak can either give life, healing, and encouragement, or they can cause death, trials, sorrows, or destruction. Words have that kind of power. Words can heal, and words can hurt. The words we speak are released into the atmosphere where the powers and principalities of the air are searching for an opportunity to pick up a word weapon to use against people and nations. These words form thoughts designed to set notions, lies, and declarations of deception into the minds of people. The enemy now takes an advanced step and stirs up a person's emotions, causing them to become rifled, which causes them to act on the notions of lies and deceptions while convincing the person these lies are true when, in fact, they are lies.

At one time or another, we have all been accused of doing and saying things we've never done or said. I've seen relationships torn apart because of the choice of words spoken in the heat of the moment. I've seen a person's character shredded by someone who was not ready to deal with the message of truth given to them. We forget that God told us to treat each other the way we want to be treated, and Satan laughs and taunts each moment we do.

Satan knows how to play against our emotions and our weaknesses to achieve his goal, which is rendering the body of Christ ineffective in their testimony, causing discord in the church, and hindering us from walking in the authority God gives us to operate in the kingdom of heaven. The adage "The devil made me do it" doesn't really hold true. Satan can set everything up and cause us to think we have no other choice but to follow through with the way the current situation is unfolding and pressure us to act in accordance with his plan, but we have the power to choose. We have the power within us to put the devil in his place and live a victorious life, walking in the light of God's salvation.

God tells us no weapon formed against us will prosper, any word spoken against us will be shown to be wrong, and we must let Satan know we know this. Just tell him, "No! You must go!" We must know who we are in Christ. Ask God to guide you into His truth. Ask God to show you the right decisions to make and the right direction to turn. Ask God to give you the strength to change what is within your ability to change and the wisdom to know what to leave in God's hands.

People are getting discouraged and becoming weary from being beaten down by opposition they are not even aware of because they are unwilling to accept God's complete message to His children. Knowledge is power. When you make a mistake, stop and ask God's forgiveness. Don't beat yourself up (Satan wants you to do this). Learn from the mistake and go forward (this really frustrates Satan). Satan is defeated by the blood of the Lamb and the word of our testimony (Revelation 12:11).

Put On Your Armor

We are in a race, and we should run this race to win (1 Corinthians 9:24). "I press on to reach the end of the race and receive the heavenly prize for which God, through Christ Jesus, is calling us" (Philippians 3:14, NLT). In order to be properly engaged in spiritual warfare, we must be armed with the weapons of this warfare (2 Corinthians 10:4–5) by putting on the whole armor of God every day (Ephesians 6:10–18), knowing who we are in Christ and the authority given to us for being God's child (Ephesians 2:4–10), studying God's Word to know about matters pertaining to us and the world around us, and then combating the lies by speaking the truth in God's Word (2 Timothy 3:16–17). We use God's mighty weapons, not worldly weapons, to knock down the devil's strongholds, for the devil roams around like a roaring lion seeking anyone he can devour (1

Peter 5:8–10). Satan knows his eternal destination will be the burning lake of fire. Satan's mission is to keep as many people out of heaven as he can in the time he has left on this earth. His focus is to render Christians ineffective in standing in their God-given authority on this earth.

> Be strong in the Lord and in his mighty power. Put on all of God's armor so that you will be able to stand firm against all strategies of the devil. For we are not fighting against flesh-and-blood enemies, but against evil rulers and authorities of the unseen world, against mighty powers in this dark world, and against evil spirits in the heavenly places.

> Ephesians 6:10–12 (NLT)

Verse 12 plainly tells us the conflict we are in is spiritual in nature.

Use every piece of God's armor to resist the enemy in the time of evil so that after the battle you will still be standing firm (Ephesians 6:13). Humble ourselves and submit to God and resist the devil and he will flee (James

4:7). According to Scripture, even the demons shake in fear of God (James 2:9). When we come into agreement with God and speak His Word, the power of God's Word goes forth and will accomplish all God sends it out to accomplish. Satan will try to convince you this will not work, but after all, he is the father of all lies.

> Stand your ground, putting on the belt of truth and the body armor of God's righteousness. For shoes, put on the peace that comes from the Good News so that you will be fully prepared. In addition to all of these, hold up the shield of faith to stop the fiery arrows of the devil. Put on salvation as your helmet, and take the sword of the Spirit, which is the word of God.

Ephesians 6:14–17 (NLT)

Put on the belt of truth. Satan is the "father of all lies," and lying lips are detestable to God (Proverbs 6:16–17); having truth is a necessary weapon of warfare. Jesus is the way, the truth, and the life (John 14:6), and the only way we can come to God is through Jesus Christ. Truth is of utmost importance in the life of a Christian. Without truth, the rest of the armor would be of no use because God's truth, the foundation of our belief, sets us free (John 8:32). The belt was the first thing a Roman soldier put on when dressing for battle. This belt held all his weapons for battle in place, ready for his use. The first piece of armor we should put on every day is studying God's truth found in His Word. His truth in us keeps us strong and ready for battle. God's truth is our foundation in waging effective warfare against the enemy.

Put on the breastplate of righteousness. A breastplate shields a warrior's vital organs from blows that would otherwise be fatal. Our righteousness is the righteousness of Christ that is given to us by God through faith and belief in Christ Jesus, which guards our hearts against the accusations, lies, and attacks of Satan and gives us assurance we never battle alone.

For shoes, put on the gospel of peace. The gospel is the foundation of our faith, giving us a firm foundation for facing spiritual battles. Knowing the gospel of peace will keep your feet firmly planted against the threats and lies of the enemy, against false doctrines, and it will keep us steady in the heat of the battle through changing seasons.

Holding up the shield of faith causes the fiery darts of doubt and fear that tell us God is not faithful and His Word is not true to be extinguished. Faith gives us the confidence and strength to persevere. Jesus Christ is the author and finisher of our faith (Hebrews 12:2), and He is a shield around us. Imagine yourself inside a huge bubble. You see large, fiery arrows coming at you in an attack launched against you. The arrows bounce off this bubble, are extinguished, and fall away. Not one of them can penetrate this bubble of protection around you. Holding up the shield of faith protects you the same way. Psalm 91 paints a clear picture of how God protects us. Holding firm to the shield of faith keeps those fiery arrows from harming us.

The helmet of salvation protects our minds from the attacks of Satan aimed to cause us to doubt the security of our salvation and the care of our heavenly Father. Too many Christians have given up the authority God has given them and have no foundation of confidence because they do not stand against the lies and deceptions of Satan.

The sword of the Spirit is the Word of God. God's Word is the powerful weapon that will destroy every form of bondage and set the captive free. God's Word is the two-edged sword revealing His glory as He uses it as a sword of judgment (in the courtroom of heaven) against Satan. When Jesus was tempted in the wilderness, it was God's Word Jesus spoke to come against the lies and temptations of Satan. God's Word is life to all our flesh and the weapon of our warfare that calms our doubts and fears. Isaiah 14:16 (NLT) tells us, "Everyone there will stare at you and ask, 'Can this be the one who shook the earth and made the kingdoms of the world tremble?'" Although he can cause a lot of destruction, Satan is not all he thinks he is. God is much more powerful—in fact, all-powerful. Don't give in to his fear tactics. We have the power to put him in his place by speaking God's Word. God said, "If my people, who are called by my name, will humble themselves and pray and seek my face and turn from their wicked ways, then I will hear from heaven, and I will forgive their sin and will heal their land" (2 Chronicles 7:14, NIV). Satan has worked very hard to keep God's people out of God's Word because Satan knows he is defeated by the blood of the Lamb and the word of our testimony (Revelation 12:11).

Stand Firm—Watch and Pray

If there were no opposition, no adversary, then living the life of a Christian on this earth would be like "heaven on earth." On the flip side, because we obviously know life on this earth can have many troubles and heartaches, some might say we are living in hell on this earth, and when the end of this earth as we know it comes, we will all go to heaven. Both modes of thinking, according to Scripture, are incorrect.

Heaven is a real place.

> Don't let your hearts be troubled. Trust in God, and trust also in me. There is more than enough room in my Father's home. If this were not so, would I have told you that I am going to prepare a place for you? When everything is ready, I will come and get you, so that you will always be with me where I am.

John 14:1–3 (NLT)

Hell is also a real place. "And these will go away into eternal punishment, but the righteous into eternal life" (Matthew 25:46, ESV). "They will throw them into the blazing furnace, where there will be weeping and gnashing of teeth" (Matthew 13:42, NIV). Heaven is a place where "He will wipe away all tears from their eyes, and there shall be no more death, nor sorrow, nor crying, nor pain. All of that has gone forever" (Revelation 21:4, TLB). Heaven is reserved for those who have stayed the course of the race and finished the race, holding fast to their faith that Jesus is the Son of God and has forgiven them of their sins. Hell is a place reserved for Satan himself, all his demons, and all those who refused to accept the sacrifice Christ made on the cross of Calvary for the atonement of their sin.

We are in a race. Run this race to win it. When we do, we will receive the crown of life that we will place at the feet of Jesus. Satan knows this truth. We, as children of the Most High God, must know this truth too. "Therefore, put on every piece of God's armor so you will be able to resist the enemy in the time of evil. Then after the battle you will still be standing firm" (Ephesians 6:13, NLT). "Pray in the

Spirit at all times and on every occasion. Stay alert and be persistent in your prayers for all believers everywhere" (Ephesians 6:18, NLT). Sometimes, the trials come at us like endless waves of suffering and struggles. Sometimes, you may not have the strength to pray. Even so, during these times, don't bow out. Don't give up. Continue to speak God's Word and praise God for who He is, all that He has done, and all He promises to do. "The praises of our fathers surrounded your throne; they trusted you and you delivered them" (Psalm 22:3–4, TLB). Understand that it is God's anointing (His power) that destroys the bondages of God's people (Isaiah 10:27). God cannot lie, and He cannot fail.

As God's representatives on earth, we have the right to exercise power over the powers and principalities of this world. "I have given you authority over all the power of the enemy" (Luke 10:19, TLB). We partner with God to stand against the evil on this earth and spread the gospel of Jesus Christ to all nations. In order to win the war you are engaged in, you must be properly prepared. The battle belongs to the Lord, and He fights even when we are calm, but it is fought through speaking God's Word in the authority of our prayers. Choosing to speak God's Word in the name of Jesus Christ releases God's power to accomplish His perfect will.

Satan has been defeated by the work of the cross of Calvary and the power that raised Jesus from the grave, which has overcome sin and death. "How we thank God for all of this! It is he who makes us victorious through Jesus Christ our Lord" (1 Corinthians 15:57, TLB). There is power in prayer. Confess your sins and pray for each other so that you may be healed. "The earnest prayer of a righteous person has great power and produces wonderful results" (James 5:16, NLT). Don't give up. Only a little bit of faith is needed for God to do something great! Jesus tells us to take heart, for He has overcome the world. When we continue to walk in God's love and exercise the authority He gives us, we will continue to grow and walk in the light of His salvation.

Time of Reflection

Be alert and of sober mind. Your enemy the devil prowls around like a roaring lion looking for someone to devour. Resist him, standing firm in the faith.

1 Peter 5:8–9 (NIV)

List three things you discovered about Satan.

Read James 2:19. Does knowing this help you stand in the authority God has given you? Discuss ways you can lessen the opportunities for Satan to come against you in your life.

Read Deuteronomy 1:21. What lands has God told you to take possession of? How will you do this?

Take the time to pray and ask God to help you stand against the attacks of Satan. Ask God to give you strength to stand in your authority, knowing He will always defend you.

Chapter 8

Authority Over Mind and Flesh

For to set the mind on the flesh is death, but to set the mind on the Spirit is life and peace.

Romans 8:6 (ESV)

The Flesh—Is It Only Skin Deep?

Our flesh, as referred to in Scripture, is our physical nature, our body, and all its parts that function in the physical realm of life. Our flesh is also referred to as our sin nature. We are born with the natural disposition to sin against God. This happens before we are given the opportunity to do anything. Although we are taught to make good choices for ourselves, the Bible tells us those who are under the control of the flesh cannot please God (Romans

8:8). The Bible also says those who live according to the flesh and who never desire change or repent from their sinful behavior will experience separation from God, both in this life and the next.

> Don't be misled; remember that you can't ignore God and get away with it: A man will always reap just the kind of crop he sows! If he sows to please his own wrong desires, he will be planting seeds of evil and he will surely reap a harvest of spiritual decay and death; but if he plants the good things of the Spirit, he will reap the everlasting life that the Holy Spirit gives him.

> Galatians 6:7–8 (TLB)

Our only hope is Jesus.

So, why do we see such a disarray of injustices in today's world? Because obeying the flesh causes us to disobey God's Word. Where flesh abounds, sin abounds. But, where sin abounds, grace abounds (Romans 5:21); the grace that is greater than all our sin.

And we have received God's Spirit (not the world's spirit), so we can know the wonderful things God has freely given us. When we tell you these things, we do not use words that come from human wisdom. Instead, we speak words given to us by the Spirit, using the Spirit's words to explain spiritual truths.

1 Corinthians 2:12–13 (NLT)

Should we continue to sin so that grace will abound even more? By no means! (Romans 6:1). If we live by the flesh, we will die, but if we live by the Spirit and put to death the deeds of the flesh, we will live (Romans 8:13). Walk led by the Holy Spirit, and you will not gratify the desires of the flesh (Galatians 5:16). When we rely on the Spirit of the Lord, we have what is necessary to overcome the sins of the flesh and injustices in this world.

For example, a child acts in the flesh when they sneak a cookie out of the cookie jar right before dinner even after being told not to do so. Our flesh is played against our emotions and is what tells us to verbally lash out at others when things are said or done that offend us, regardless of how it affects the other person. Our flesh is what tells us it is okay to spitefully use others to get a job promotion. Our flesh is what causes us to defy the trust of a close relationship and lie about who we were out with the night before. Our flesh convinces us there is nothing wrong with having sex with someone before marriage even though God has clearly told us to abstain for our own good (1 Corinthians 6:18–19, Matthew 5:27–28, Proverbs 14:12). Our flesh will disgrace our brother or sister for a sin they have committed when "they certainly knew better" while putting themselves on a pedestal saying, "I've never done that!" Our flesh shows itself in many ways. Our flesh is what sets a whirlwind of destructive vices into play against what God has determined is His best for us. Our flesh works against the Spirit of God in us and demands its own way.

Through our flesh and the battle within our minds, the war against us is waged to keep us from maintaining a close relationship with God. Satan knows our weaknesses and will use any opportunity given to him to use those weaknesses against us and others to undermine the work of the Lord. We are different, and we will disagree to some extent. There is nothing wrong with disagreeing; however, behavior becomes inappropriate when disagreements are expressed in a destructive manner. There seems to be no shortage of those who feel it is their duty to point out your shortcomings and even give you credit for everything gone wrong. Many years ago, after the onslaught of someone's blame game, a very dear friend of mine told me, "Even a clock that is broken and no longer working is still right twice a day." Never forget it.

God tells us to live in peace with one another with gentleness and self-control (Galatians 5:23, Hebrews 12:14, Colossians 3:15, 2 Corinthians 13:11, Romans 12:18). Be encouraged and put on love.

We Shall Overcome

I have heard it said, "Use moderation in all things." God tells us we can do anything we want to do if Christ has not said no—that is, if God's word has not said no.

Since some of these things are not good for us, wisdom should step in and tell us not to do those things that we might not be able to easily stop when we want to stop them (1 Corinthians 6:12). Knowing we have a flesh obstacle does not mean we must be enslaved to it. Instead, we are to crucify our flesh. "I have been crucified with Christ and I no longer live, but Christ lives in me. The life I now live in the body, I live by faith in the Son of God, who loved me and gave himself for me" (Galatians 2:20, NIV). When Christ gave His life for us, He cleansed all our sins through shedding His blood, including the sins of our flesh. Although we are still capable of sinning, through grace, we can overcome the deeds of the flesh through the power of God working in us. Crucifying our flesh means making our flesh come into obedience to the Word of God and the ways of Christ.

To overcome the flesh, we must come into agreement with God that there are areas of our lives we need to change. "If we say that we have no sin, we are only fooling ourselves and refusing to accept the truth" (1 John 1:8, TLB). Reading and meditating on God's Holy Scriptures helps us overcome the desires of the flesh. We are known for our fruits (Matthew 7:16), but the fruit of the Spirit is love, joy, peace, patience, kindness, goodness, faithfulness, gentleness, and self-control (Galatians 5:22–23). I heard a pastor tell the story of when the temptation to sin was presented to him. He confronted it and immediately left the opportunity that was enticing him as Joseph ran away from Potiphar's wife's advances. He said, "If you don't embarrass sin, sin's gonna embarrass you!" We are all tempted to give in to the desires of the flesh. Acting on those temptations is what causes us to sin and not walk in God's best for us.

I knew of a woman who was struggling to overcome physical illness and the onslaught of difficulties associated with it while raising three children as a single parent. The doubts, fears, and feelings of failure only served to compound exhaustion while working tirelessly to meet their physical needs. What made this more difficult were those who could not see past where her current circumstances held her, being convinced they were earned by her due to sin, and they offered no sense of relief. This added flame to the fire of the opposition she faced and deepened the wounds of defeat. The Word of God tells us to help those in trouble, then your light will shine out from the darkness, and the darkness around you will be as bright as the noon-day sun (Isaiah 58:10).

> And so, from the day we heard, we have not ceased to pray for you, asking that you may be filled with the knowledge of his will in all spiritual wisdom and understanding, so as to walk in a manner worthy of the Lord, fully pleasing to him: bearing fruit in every good work and increasing in the knowledge of God; being strengthened with all power, according to his glorious might, for all endurance and patience with joy; giving thanks to the Father, who has qualified you to share in the inheritance of the saints in light. He has delivered us from the domain of darkness and transferred us to the kingdom of his beloved Son, in whom we have redemption, the forgiveness of sins.

Colossians 1:9–14 (ESV)

Jesus said, "By this everyone will know that you are

my disciples, if you love one another" (John 13:35, NIV).
The world we live in will never run short of opportunities
to tempt our flesh to raise itself against God. Overcoming
the deeds of the flesh is not always a simple endeavor;
however, all things are possible with God (Mark 10:27).
Trust Him. Greater is he who is in us than he who is in the
world (1 John 4:4).

For as a Man Thinks, So Is He

Our minds are where the seeds of corruption are
planted. Sinful thoughts are something all believers struggle
with from time to time. We cannot control all thoughts that
pop into our minds, but we can control how we respond to
these thoughts. Second Corinthians 10:15 tells us to take
every thought captive and make it obedient to Christ. Why
is it important we take every thought captive?

In the movie *Facing the Giants*, a father encourages his
son to succeed by believing he can succeed. [11] Our beliefs
begin with the thoughts in our minds. Our thoughts lead to
the words we speak. James 3:4 says our tongues are like the
rudder on a ship—very small but able to move a whole ship

into the direction it steers. Our tongue can set many things in motion by the words we speak—whether good or bad. Jesus said that the things that come out of the mouth come from the heart and that these things make a man unclean (Matthew 15:18). So, now we are back to how our words have power. And they start with the thoughts in our minds.

If we dwell on good, positive things, those thoughts will get in our hearts, and we will speak about the good, positive things. When we speak positive things into our lives, we maintain peace in our minds. Even though things around us may seem like they are falling apart, we can maintain the mental hope that in all things, God works all things together for our good (Romans 8:28). God's Word is life to all our flesh. When we speak life into our situation and into our hearts, it opens the door for God to work all things together for His purpose.

If we dwell on negative things, likewise, those thoughts will get in our hearts, and we will speak about the negative things. Before you know it, you will find something negative about everything and everyone you see. In turn, what started as a simple thought has now turned our lives into believing the desperate notion that things will never get better. Our happiness and mental well-being start with our thought life.

A person can be blessed with an abundance of wealth, esteem, and camaraderie the lifestyle can bring, but be trapped in the loneliness of their minds with thoughts of "who's out to get me next." I knew a man who had a brilliant intellect and could quote facts like reading an encyclopedia. Because of childhood abuse and emotional neglect, low self-esteem developed. This, in turn, caused a mental stronghold to develop (a false belief), and insecurities caused him to overcompensate with his intelligence. He became egotistical and domineering. He became someone who abused others, only with increased intensity than what he himself endured.

Mental strongholds can convince a person the only viable choice in an unplanned pregnancy is to have an abortion, which ultimately causes more grief and despair due to the loss of a child—a far cry from the abundant life God promises us through Christ.

People can find themselves in physical prisons for a

wide variety of reasons. With time on their hands, they
have many opportunities to think about what they did.
To maintain mental clarity, guiding their thoughts toward
making better choices allows them the mental freedom to
hope for a brighter future. On the flip side, there are many
who are imprisoned due to no fault of their own except for
being lured by deceptive measures, such as kidnapping
or human trafficking. The fear and desperation they face
is beyond comprehension. They are quickly thrust into
a situation where they fight to maintain mental sanity to
survive.

Many who have mental illness and those with special
needs are often grossly misunderstood as they struggle
to overcome being imprisoned in their minds or bodies.
They can be an easy target for those who are unkind
and insensitive. Too often, they find themselves unable
to process the rejection of others, and being unable to
cope any longer, they contemplate suicide. In any case, a
person's mind can be their best friend or their worst enemy.

Regardless of a person's condition in life, because we
are made in the likeness of God and our lives are a gift

from the Maker above, we should treat others with dignity. In a world where we are often overlooked, take comfort in knowing there is one who knows where you are, knows everything about you, and still loves you the most in any circumstance. That person is Jesus Christ, the One who loved you before others ever knew you.

Of the many roads traveled, our minds will either bring us out or bury us deeper within. Whether we come through good or bad circumstances or have little or much, God has great plans for us and places great value on us because we are His creation. Everything good comes from the Lord's hand. To find peace and deliverance, we must learn to set our minds on things above and have compassion for others. "For God has not given us a spirit of fear, but of power and of love and of a sound mind" (2 Timothy 1:7, NKJV). In my lifetime, I have had much, and I have had almost nothing. I have learned to be content either way because my hope is built on Jesus Christ, the very life of my existence.

"Finally, brothers and sisters, whatever is true, whatever is noble, whatever is right, whatever is pure, whatever is lovely, whatever is admirable—if anything is excellent or praiseworthy—think about such things" (Philippians 4:8, NIV). This does not promote, as some might say, the power of positive thinking; it simply means we have a choice. We are encouraged to maintain good thoughts in our thinking. We are given many opportunities to think about things that are difficult or grievous. We, however, do not have to allow negative thoughts to control us. "Your attitude should be the kind that was shown us by Jesus Christ" (Philippians 2:5, TLB)

In my personal walk, I ask the Lord to help me bridle my tongue and guide conversations. I also ask Him to help me bridle the tongue of my thoughts and give me His perspective. [12]

Renew and Refresh

"A cheerful heart does good like medicine, but a broken spirit makes one sick" (Proverbs 17:22, TLB). "Don't copy the behavior and customs of this world, but be a new and different person with a fresh newness in all you do and think. Then you will learn from your own experience how His ways will really satisfy you" (Romans 12:2, TLB).

As children, we are raised through the beliefs and thought patterns of our parents and the communities in which we are raised. In some cases, we are born into strongholds of poverty, which serve to enslave us indefinitely. Often, it is tainted by the world's measure of what is right, which gives over to the sensuality and indulgence in every kind of impurity and greed and breeds the perpetual cycle of defeat. Regardless of the past we struggled through, deliverance from the prison walls that serve to keep us bound is attainable through trusting Jesus Christ. Allow His unconditional love to deliver, heal, and transform you into the person He has created you to be. God wants us to do well and prosper. "My dear friend, I know that you are doing well spiritually. So I pray that everything else is going well with you and that you are enjoying good health" (3 John 1:2, ERV).

As a Christian,

> Since you have heard about Jesus and have learned the truth that comes from him, throw off your old sinful nature and your former way of life, which is corrupted by lust and deception.

Instead, let the Spirit renew your thoughts and
attitudes. Put on your new nature, created to be
like God—truly righteous and holy.

Ephesians 4:21–24 (NLT)

Our salvation with God is obtained through the ongoing
process of sanctification. "Sanctification" means "setting
apart persons or things to God." Sanctification is guided
by the Holy Spirit and God's Word. Build yourself up in
the most holy faith (Jude 1:20). Speak the Word of God
out loud to yourself over and over so that your ears can
hear the Word of God you are speaking so that it will enter
your heart and renew and refresh your mind, heart, and
soul. "Faith comes from hearing, and hearing through the
word of Christ" (Romans 10:17, ESV). It will be a lamp to
your feet and a light to your path (Psalm 119:105) and will
change your life.

Oh, for the joy that comes in the morning for weeping
only endures for the night (Psalm 30:5). There will be
seasons of weeping in our lives, but God promises us joy

will come. Those who sow in tears will reap songs of joy (Psalm 126:5). A harvest of good will come if we do not give up (Galatians 6:9). At each level of growth with God, we must realize our need to rely on Him, even when our lives are running smoothly. If we take our relationship with God for granted, we risk not finishing the race. Press on to endure the race set before you, and do not give up. God will never give up on us. [13]

Time of Reflection

So I say, walk by the Spirit, and you will not gratify the desires of the flesh.

Galatians 5:16 (NIV)

Discuss your opinion of what the flesh is regarding your walk with Christ. How does this affect you and those around you?

Read 2 Corinthians 10:5. How do you take every thought and make it obedient to Christ?

Compare Romans 7:15 and Galatians 5:16. What does this mean to you? Why is it important to walk by the Spirit of God?

Take the time to pray and ask God to make Himself and the Holy Spirit real to you. Ask God to make you sensitive to the Holy Spirit and His desire for your life every day.

Chapter 9

Walking in Love and Forgiveness

Above all, keep loving one another earnestly, since love
covers a multitude of sins.

1 Peter 4:8 (ESV)

Abide in His Love

We discussed in chapter 4 what God says love is as it
translates into everyday life. Agape love is always shown
by what it does. The world will know we are Christians by
our love (John 13:35). God has called us into His love for
two primary reasons: to love Him and love others (Matthew
22:37). Because we are born into human sin nature, love
does not come naturally to us. If we are to love the way
God tells us to love, we must receive this love from the

source—God.

> Dear friends, let us continue to love one another, for love comes from God. Anyone who loves is a child of God and knows God. But anyone who does not love does not know God, for God is love.
>
> God showed how much he loved us by sending his one and only Son into the world so that we might have eternal life through him. This is real love—not that we loved God, but that he loved us and sent his Son as a sacrifice to take away our sins.
>
> Dear friends, since God loved us that much, we surely ought to love each other. No one has ever seen God. But if we love each other, God lives in us, and his love is brought to full expression in us.

1 John 4:7–12 (NLT)

Our purpose on this earth is to live in a relationship with God, loving Him and loving others. Our mission is to tell the world that God loves them.

If I speak in the tongues of men or of angels, but do not have love, I am only a resounding gong or a clanging cymbal. If I have the gift of prophecy and can fathom all mysteries and all knowledge, and if I have a faith that can move mountains, but do not have love, I am nothing. If I give all I possess to the poor and give over my body to hardship that I may boast, but do not have love, I gain nothing.

1 Corinthians 13:1–3 (NIV)

We can obtain all the good this world can give, but if we do not have love, our lives will become empty, and the longings of our souls will remain unfulfilled.

Love can be expressed by others in many ways. Physical needs, for example, groceries, can be met through the act of someone showing a person love and giving them groceries. Now, love has met a need. However, physical needs will need to be replenished. When we hear that someone has suffered a tragic loss, people gather to offer condolences to buffer the shock and ease the intense pain of loss. This can last for days, weeks, or longer, but eventually, the visits and calls will lessen over time, and the person grieving is still left to carry on with the emptiness of this loss within them. There are no words we can say and nothing we can do to bring complete healing. It is not humanly possible to fill this void. There is only one person who can understand the inner workings of our being in an intimate way and sustain the longings of the soul, and that person is Jesus Christ. Real love is something that cannot be bought or sold. It cannot be obtained through simply the desire to have it. Love is what completes us as human beings. Love is how the world will know we are Christians—it is what sets us apart from every other religion in the world because of the very nature of what love is.

After leaving an abusive marriage, I felt alone and completely unlovable. In fact, I could not remember who I was before I got married. What I needed more than any-thing was to know if God still loved me. For me to come to that place, I needed to be restored with gentleness and love. I was fortunate to be in a church who showed me love and support, and I had friends who helped me through my journey of recovery. I had put up so many walls of defense to survive, I had a very hard time allowing anyone to get close to me. But God… God rescued me. I came to know God's unconditional love for me during those long, lonely nights when no one else was there but God. No one else but God knew every abusive action and every ill-spoken word purposed against me. And in every moment, it was God and only God who knew how to speak to my heart and soul. God's love and what His love did in me gave me the strength to go forward and become who I am today—whole and complete in Christ Jesus. No one else but God understands the condition of the human soul. No one else but God knows the beat of every heart. No one else but God knows how to speak the words that will set you free and make you whole.

Loving others does not mean you are expected to open the door of your life and allow anyone who happens along to come in and take up residence. We teach our children not to open the door to strangers. Sometimes, we need to heed this lesson as well. Matthew 7:6 (NIV) tells us, "Do not give dogs what is sacred; do not throw your pearls to pigs.

If you do, they may trample them under their feet, and turn and tear you to pieces." We are to show everyone love and be respectful, but we are to use wisdom. Allowing wolves in sheep's clothing to take up residence in our goodness and kindness will only serve to tear us down. God tells us to cast our cares on Him and to not get weary in well-doing, but He also tells us we are not to be a doormat for those sent to suck the life out of us—use discernment. Admitting we are not the chosen person to minister to someone is not a weakness. It is called using wisdom. God expects us to guard our hearts while we minister to the hearts of others.

God knows our hearts. He knows our motives. Do we love only when convenient for us? Do we show love only when it complements what we hope to achieve from it? God's love in us allows us to love those who have who have spitefully used us, turned their backs on us, abused us, or spoken lies about us. God tells us to love others just as He has loved us. A true act of loving with God's love is telling someone that Jesus loves them too. God's love sets us free. God's love will stand the test of time.

Offense Is Not Mine to Take

Walking in forgiveness is not always an easy task. However, it is an extension of walking in love with one another. In the world we live in, we are given many opportunities to become hurt and offended by what others say or do. We are human and have our own opinions. They are often not like everyone else. It never seems to fail; in a moment of weakness someone somewhere is unable to resist the urge to express those opinions—strongly. It helps to remember we are not alone in our efforts to stand up for truth. God is always by our side. It also helps to remember Satan knows our weaknesses and makes it his business to work against them as often as he can to cause strife and unrest. What do you do when your opposition is abrasive? Blessed are the meek for theirs in the kingdom of heaven (Matthew 5:3). Meekness does not mean weakness, nor does it mean we are not to take decisive action against wrong when necessary. Meekness is power under control. It takes a lot of strength and determination to refuse to take offense and walk in forgiveness. "Because the Sovereign Lord helps me, I will not be disgraced. Therefore, I have set my face like a stone, determined to do his will. And I know that I will not be put to shame" (Isaiah 50:7, NLT). Through the power of God's love in us, we are given the ability to rise above offense.

Divide and conquer is the policy of maintaining control over one's subordinates or followers by encouraging dissent and division between them. Satan is the ruler of the powers and principalities of this world. Divide and conquer is something Satan loves to do—in relationships, families, nations, and in the body of Christ. Offense is easily inflated when problems arise. We do not have to take offense. Offense comes from Satan to cause division and strife. Offense is like rubbing salt in a wound to keep the pain alive, which causes it to fester into a boil. Offense becomes a root of bitterness within our soul and negatively affects every relationship and interaction we have with others. Our emotions take over, and we make decisions based on those emotions instead of God's truth. If you do not think Satan is actively working against us and our churches, think again. This is one thing he does best. We, as God's children, must stand and take authority against this. Would you sit idle and not take decisive action against a thief who broke into your house to rob you? Of course not! Forgiving one another and showing God's love through the fault will quickly deflate the work of Satan.

Forgiveness can be difficult when injustices are committed against us by those who are driven by a cold, callous heart. However, we do not get to choose who and what we will forgive. We are commanded by God to forgive, even when others never admit they have done anything wrong. This is also a true act of love.

I heard a story of a woman who was raised in a good, loving home by parents who were not actively serving Christ. Through involvement in a local youth ministry, she herself accepted Christ as her Savior. This woman described many experiences she had in several churches as she grew in her faith. She recounted hearing leadership arguing loudly behind closed doors about how a service should be run, minutes before it began. She described another instance when she was lured by deception into a situation that caused her to be brutally attacked. Compassion was not shown to her by those with whom she attended church. They instead shunned her. When these events caused her to question her own faith, she was met with disregard. She allowed offense and hurt to take root, and she ultimately walked away from the Christian faith entirely. In this instance, we find a woman who was deeply hurt. She allowed the hurt to become a root of bitterness in her soul. Instead of leaning on God and trusting His love for her and His ability to bring people into her life to help her, she chose to walk away. What a travesty! All too often, Satan's ploys and tactics take their toll when we choose not to forgive and love beyond the faults.

There are many people in the church who are hurting from wounds that have never fully healed. Those in leadership can become overwhelmed with the task of fulfilling God's vision in their ministry. There is a tendency to put church leaders on a pedestal, and then disillusionment sets in when they do not measure up to the man-made standard set for them. Jesus is our Savior. God is our source, and we are all in need of prayer. Only God can pick up the shattered pieces of our lives and put them together to make the beautiful picture of hope we need and desire.

"Judge not" is a two-way street. Loving one another is a two-way street. We can stay mad at God, and we can stay mad at others, but there will come a day when we will meet our Maker and will answer to Him for everything we did, even what we allowed in our thoughts. Jesus said to those who were weary and heavily burdened to go to Him that He will give them rest (Matthew 11:28). If we look to others for our direction, hope, peace, and healing, we will always be sorely dissatisfied and in doing so, many will become disillusioned with the Christian faith. Discover the source of offense at its root, and then go to your source, who is the God of deliverance. Purpose in your heart not to take offense, stand on God's Word to set you free, and always look to God, who will always work things together for your good.

Our lives are God's gift to us. What we work to accomplish and how we live our lives is our gift to God. Forgiving someone means letting them, and yourself, know your life does not belong to them, and you are declaring you will not allow the pain caused by that person to control your life. Walking in forgiveness with someone does not negate the wrong they did. It simply gives you the freedom to move forward.

Forgiveness is not always as simple as saying we will do it and accomplishing it just by saying it. Forgiveness can be a process. It can be difficult to forgive someone whose purpose in their lives is to speak and spread lies about your character, especially when they refuse to admit wrongdoing themselves. Interestingly, this can come from those who do not know you and have never had a conversation with you. I have found some of my biggest struggles came in forgiving myself for the wrongdoings I did. It forced me to look deeper within myself to understand why I made the choices I made. This can be a very difficult and painful process, but through this, we find safety in the arms of God's love and experience God's faithfulness to restore our souls (Psalm 23:3). Forgive the offense. Release the offense to God's capable hands to handle and ask Him to fill you up to love again. [14]

Love That Restores

Sometimes, we can get stuck thinking that we have gone too far or that there is no hope. The foundation of the Christian faith is based on relationships. Jesus did not come to save the righteous. He came to save the sinner. The very definition of a relationship describes the involvement of more than one person. Through Christ, God has reconciled us into a relationship with Him. In turn, we have been given the ministry of reconciliation to lead others to Christ (2 Corinthians 5:8). Regardless of how noble a person is, they still have feet of clay. No one makes it across the finish line of a race on someone else's effort. Each of us must put in the work to be transformed into the image of Christ. Working out our own salvation is never a one-way street. It is always a give and take. Truth is always a two-edged sword, which cuts through the maze of short-sightedness and deception that raises its head to fuel complacency, division, hurt, and strife to breed contempt against the people in this world.

We are in a race against time, and our battle is against

the one who does not want to see peace on this earth. When we refuse to acknowledge all the factors that are involved in the work against us, we might as well be putting our heads in the sand. The current human condition of man cannot be explained away by a simple "He should have, but she didn't." We all come to the table with certain expectations and there is not one single kitchen able to satisfy every taste. Yet, according to Scripture, there are clear guidelines on how we are each supposed to act.

We are not all cut from the same cloth. We all come from different backgrounds, and we all filter our opinions through those experiences. Some, thankfully, have never experienced major life-changing traumas. Therefore, they may find it difficult to understand the condition of those who have. There are some who have become burnt out in their chosen profession or calling and find themselves unable to cope. To many, this can appear as though they are always fighting against the very ones who are trying to help them. Then there are those who are sincerely trying to understand their call and purpose and cannot seem to grasp a solid concept of it due to the brokenness of those who are supposed to lead the way. Too many times, we cast our complaints against others and fail to go to God, who can make everything change.

How often do we pray first for those who hurt us instead of criticizing them? Why do we feel it is left up to us to handle everything and not go boldly to the throne room first to find mercy and grace in our time of need and trust God with it? Are there injustices against God in the church? Unfortunately, yes. Are there broken people who are rigidly short-sighted and who give up and walk away without likewise following the commands of God to come to Him first and allow God to work? Unfortunately, yes. Why are we not standing up and shouting out loud, "Satan! You have to go!" We are all in need of a Savior. We are all made with feet of clay!

"So when we preach that Christ was crucified, the Jews are offended and the Gentiles say it's all nonsense. But to those called by God to salvation, both Jews and Gentiles, Christ is the power of God and the wisdom of God" (1 Corinthians 1:23–24, NLT). There is no one righteous. No not one (Romans 3:10). Judging someone based on what they do while judging yourself based on your idea of right is a disaster waiting to happen. We are in this world but not of it. This is true. But the reality is, we are all affected by it. If the evil in this world is offered and accepted by others it will cause disaster and heartache to masses. God wants to restore us all to wholeness from the broken condition we find ourselves in, and He will for those who allow Him to do so. If you do not find the answers you need right away, never stop searching. God will reward those who diligently seek Him (Hebrews 11:6).

God tells us He will restore the good things that have been stolen from us (Joel 2:25–32). Mercy triumphs over judgment (James 2:13). When we accept and receive this for ourselves, we find the peace that only He can give. A very dear friend, who was wise in his perceptions, always had a memorable expression to describe the tides of life. He would say, "If should've, could've, and would've was candy, and it was Christmas, we'd all be happy." How true this is. We have all had disappointments—some by our own doing and some by absolutely no fault of our own. We all wish we could go back and change the mistakes we made.

Although we cannot do this, God can and will breathe life into healing our hopes and dreams and the desires of our hearts in our families, our churches, and our nation around the world. He will restore all things into something good. All things are possible with God, and all things are possible for those who believe. We need to show the love of Christ and be an encouragement to those who are hurting. The good word or smile you give someone who has become discouraged or disheartened may be the only encouragement they hear.

God proved His love for us in that Christ died for us even while we were still sinners (Romans 5:8). The ground is level at the cross of Calvary, and there is room for everyone. When we experience God's love, we are forever changed.

Strength to Release

Release. The very act of letting go. "Take delight in the Lord, and he will give you the desires of your heart" (Psalm 37:4, NIV). However, God's desires for us are not always the same as the desires we have for ourselves. His ways are higher than our ways. His thoughts are higher than our thoughts (Isaiah 55:8–9). Yet, for us to walk in the light of His salvation, our actions and thoughts have to line up with His desires.

Our walk with Christ is always balanced with receiving and releasing. To receive from God, we have to be willing to release something back to Him—whether it is the faith to take one more step or the baggage of hurt, disappointments, shortcomings, doubts, or fears. If we allow ourselves to hold on to baggage, we will not have room to receive the healing and restoration God wants to give us. We are in a relationship with Him. Relationships cannot be one-sided, or they will not grow. God loves us just the way we are. Release any thought that suggests God cannot be moved with compassion for us or that it is impossible to have a close relationship with Him.

Honor refers to the value we place on something or someone. We demonstrate this by the attention we give them and the place we give them in our lives. We are to honor God for all He has done for us. Honoring God is shown by keeping Him first in our lives and acknowledging

Him in all our ways.

In the game of football, the objective is to get the ball into the end zone—touchdown. The team with the most points wins the game. Those who have played the game know the key to getting the football to its desired location is in how you advance the ball. It is best achieved with a combination of advancement and protection. The quarterback and receiver work together to advance the ball. The offensive lineman also works to advance the ball by blocking the defensive team's efforts to prevent them from scoring. While the offensive lineman blocks the opposition's advance, the quarterback is given the clearance to throw the football to the receiver, who then carries the ball into the end zone. Touchdown! The same is true in our walk with the Lord. You and the Holy Spirit are like the quarterback and receiver. God sends you His word through the Holy Spirit and tells you the direction you should go. You receive that word and advance in the direction God sends you. God's angels and prayer warriors are like the offensive lineman. They work to block Satan's effort to keep you from succeeding in your mission of advancing the kingdom of heaven. Release your will to God. Following the leadership of the Holy Spirit is always best.

If our true desire is to delight ourselves in the Lord, we must be willing to hold lightly our plans, hopes, and dreams. God's call on our lives is irrevocable, meaning He will not change His mind. However, the manifestation of what that will look like may change due to changes in seasons of time. This is not to say we should not maintain forward motion in achieving our goals. It simply means we must be willing to release them to God. Otherwise, obtaining our goals can become the object of our desires, when reaching for a closer walk with God should be our main objective. If we want God's best for us, we will wait on Him and trust Him for what it should be. God knows how to bring it about. Doing our part is being diligent to trust Him even when nothing makes sense. Eventually, both sets of plans become the same, and we will get the desires of our hearts.

God tells us to cast our cares to the Lord, and He will not allow us to slip and fall (Psalm 55:22). Releasing is the willing act of relinquishing control. Releasing allows us to be teachable, changeable, and flexible. In doing so, we become clay in the potter's hand, and we can be transformed into the likeness of Christ.

When we release hurt, we receive healing. When we release worry, we receive peace. When we release unforgiveness, we receive more of God's power working in us and through us. When we release our faith, we release God's ability to do supernatural things for us and for others.[15]

In John 21:15–17, Jesus asked Peter three times if he loved Him. Three times, Peter answered yes. Each time, Jesus told Peter to feed and take care of His sheep. When we release ourselves and everything pertaining to our lives to the Lord, we become less, and He becomes more and greater is He who is in us than he who is in the world. His love and affirmation give us the strength to release and the strength to carry on doing the Father's will. God's love will never be fully realized unless you are fully willing to receive it.

Time of Reflection

If anyone says "I love God," but keeps on hating his brother, he is a liar; for if he doesn't love his brother who is right there in front of him, how can he love God whom he has never seen?

1 John 4:20 (TLB)

Describe how God's love has changed your life.

Have you had to face forgiving someone who refused to acknowledge the wrong they've done? How did this affect you?

Read Mark 12:30–31. Is it difficult to love your neighbor? Why or why not?

Take the time to pray and ask God to help you walk in love and forgiveness with others.

Chapter 10

Walking in Obedience

But Samuel replied, "What is more pleasing to the Lord: your burnt offerings and sacrifices or your obedience to his voice? Listen! Obedience is better than sacrifice, and submission is better than offering the fat of rams."

1 Samuel 15:22 (NLT)

We are taught at a young age there are rules to follow. We may not understand them. We may not even like them, but we are expected to live by them. We are taught that there are consequences to not obeying those rules. We teach our children to obey the boundaries that are set for them, not only to establish order in our homes but also because we know they must obey the laws of the land or end up in jail. Another reason we teach our children to be obedient is because this is what God commands of us. "Train up a child in the way he should go; even when he is old he will not depart from it" (Proverbs 22:6, ESV). "Teach [these words of mine] to your children. Talk about them when you are at home and when you are on the road, when you are going to bed and when you are getting up" (Deuteronomy 11:19, NLT). We do this so that our children will grow to be obedient to the Lord. He wants His very best for us, and He knows what lies ahead for those who refuse to obey.

Being obedient to God should not be confused with self-sacrifice as a way of earning salvation. We cannot earn our way into heaven, as we discussed previously. In return, God asks us to be obedient to the commands He has established for us. Obedience is better than sacrifice.

Being obedient to God proves our love for Him (1 John 5:2–3), demonstrates our faithfulness to Him (1 John 2:3–6), and opens the doors for more blessings for us (John 13:17). Each step of our walk with God is a stepping stone to a higher level built upon the last, and each step of obedience in Christ takes us from the valley to the highest peak. The beauty of this adventure we are on is that God does not leave us on our own to accomplish it. He leads us and guides us in the way we should go each step of the way.

Hear His Voice

> The gatekeeper opens the gate for him, and the sheep hear his voice and come to him; and he calls his own sheep by name and leads them out. He walks ahead of them; and they follow him, for they recognize his voice. They won't follow a stranger but will run from him, for they don't recognize his voice.

John 10:3–5 (TLB)

The word "hear" in this context also means "to be aware of, to perceive or be informed with understanding." Jesus tells us we, His sheep, will recognize His voice. Knowing that God speaks to us is only part of this venture. Understanding how God speaks to us is essential. God speaks to us through His Word, to our hearts, through other people, and through seeing His hand move in circumstances.

"Be still, and know that I am God!" (Psalm 46:10, NLT). Too often, we are so busy with the busyness of the day we do not slow down and be still with God. We don't take the time to seek the Lord. He tells us to seek Him while He may still be found, call on Him while He is still near (Isaiah 55:6), and when we seek Him with all our heart, surely He will be found (Jeremiah 29:13). He will reward those who earnestly seek Him (Hebrews 11:6). First Kings 19:11–13 tells us that when the prophet Elijah was seeking the Lord, God was not in whirlwind, earthquake, or fire but that God was the still small voice.

With so much going on around us, how can we be sure we are hearing God's voice? "Dear friends, do not believe everyone who claims to speak by the Spirit [of God]. You must test them to see if the spirit they have comes from God" (1 John 4:1, NLT). How do we test these spirits? There is only one way. Open the Bible and spend time with the Lord each day reading His Word. It is impossible to please God without faith. "Faith comes from hearing, that is, hearing the Good News about Christ" (Romans 10:17,

NLT). God is not going to tell you something against His Word. Take every thought captive and make it obedient to Christ, and then you will discern the paths of righteousness God is leading you on. You are less likely to take a lot of twists and turns through the valleys and more likely to stay straight on the path God is leading you on.

Remember, the weapon of our warfare is not flesh and blood. The weapon of our warfare is the sword of the Spirit through the Spirit of Truth (the Holy Spirit). "Not by force nor by strength, but by my Spirit, says the Lord" (Zechariah 4:6, NLT). Satan loves to keep God's children away from the very weapon that will render him powerless so he can gain a foothold in your life! Stop and notice how many times you have tried to spend time alone with God, but without any provocation, everything comes against that time you have set aside for Him. Staying committed to listening for His still, small voice will drown out the voice of resistance, and your ears will hear clearly what the Spirit of the Lord is saying.

"You saw me before I was born. Every day of my life was recorded in your book. Every moment was laid out before a single day had passed" (Psalm 139:16, NLT). Since God already knows what He has awaiting your arrival, it makes sense to spend time with Him to hear what He has to say. When we step out in faith in obedience to God, we now partner with Him to accomplish His perfect will in our lives. It starts with taking that first step of obedience. Work hard so God can say to you, "Well done." "Be a good workman, one who does not need to be ashamed when God examines your work. Know what his word says and means" (2 Timothy 2:15, TLB). The more time we spend with Him, the clearer His Word and direction for us become.[16]

Heed His Voice

Hearing the voice of God is only part of the battle. To achieve victory, we must also listen to His voice and put what He has told us into action. How many times do we ask someone their opinion and then quickly discount it because it was not what we wanted to hear? Faith is willing to accept God's Word as truth about everything. If we are not willing to accept His Word as truth, His Words are simply words on a page. It is not until we activate them with our faith that they become life to all our flesh. "Oh, that my people would listen to me! Oh, that Israel would follow me, walking in my paths! How quickly I would then subdue their enemies! How soon my hands would be upon their foes!" (Psalm 81:13–14, NLT). Living a life that honors God can seem frustrating with the rules and guidelines God gives us to abide by. God does not do this because He is a taskmaster given to make our lives miserable. He does this because He loves us and wants to draw closer to us. He wants to have a close personal relationship with us. He wants us to be holy people set apart for Him in every aspect of our lives. Because of Jesus Christ, we can be that holy people God desires us to be.

Our growth with the Lord requires that we continue to keep our hearts submissive to the Lord. With each level of growth, we are held to a higher standard. The more we know, the more is expected of us. If we do not continue to heed to the voice of the Lord, before we realize it, we can drift away from the Lord, and we can become like those described in Psalm 95, discontent and complaining, thinking God is ignoring us. When, in fact, God says he will never leave us or forsake us. If we become discontent, chances are we have allowed outside influences to gain a foothold in our lives. Perhaps we get restless when we are waiting for an answer from the Lord. Are you waiting well? Are you staying in God's Word, praying, and staying in fellowship with Him? Maybe the answer is slow because it is not yet time, or we are not ready to receive it. Some of God's greatest blessings are unanswered prayer. The key to understanding is listening to the voice of the Lord and submitting to His perfect will.

God is sovereign. He knows the beginning to the end. When God gives us a directive and we know we heard Him clearly, following through right away is the best plan of action. A delay can set a vast array of events in motion that will serve to keep us from gaining ground in the direction God has sent us. Faith is walking in God's plan even when the steps before you are not clearly marked. Be encouraged, and do not give place to fear. Go forward and trust God. He knows how to see you through. Look what happened to the children of Israel when they gave in to fear after the

Lord told them to take possession of the land He had given them. They ended up wandering in the desert for forty years (Numbers 14).

God tells us what is in the dark is brought to the light. There are many pitfalls waiting for us to get us off track. Because of God's steadfast love and commitment to us, He will warn His children of impending danger, but too often, we fail to heed His warnings. When our hearts long to heed the voice of the Lord, we will always be satisfied (Isaiah 58:11). The longer we serve the Lord, the more we will realize His faithfulness in caring for us.

Obey His Commands

The Lord tells us, "If you love me, you will keep my commandments" (John 14:15, ESV). Obedience to God proves our love for Him. When we are obedient to His commands, we honor Him, and through this, He is glorified, and the world will see His transforming power change us. Blessed are those who fear the Lord and walk in obedience to Him (Psalm 128:1, NIV). Walking in obedience to the Lord maintains our closeness to Him.

To hear the word and then not doing it leads to deception, but to hear the word and then doing it leads to a blessing (James 1:22–25). God tells us He is not the author of confusion and that all things are to be done decently and in order (1 Corinthians 14:33). That would include doing as He commands. Partial obedience is disobedience. Delayed obedience is disobedience. Are we willing to accept the good but not willing to be obedient to receive it? If God tells you that partaking in something specific is bad for your health and doing so will slowly kill you, yet you continue to indulge in this pleasure, are you going to get mad at God if you get sick and your body will not heal?

Maybe God has shown you the direction He wants you to go, but for whatever reason, you say, "I'm not ready." If we delay too long, although that door may not close permanently, it will likely wait for another season. Our journey with the Lord is built one step on top of another. When our steps of obedience stay in line, and in time with the Lord's commands, we will arrive at our destination as the Lord has ordained. God is never early, and He is never late. When we are following Him, we will arrive right on time.

Luke 12:42–47 tells the story of what will happen when a servant obeys his master versus one who does not. We, by virtue of our salvation, are also servants of God. There are consequences to our disobedience. Sometimes, they are realized in small ways, sometimes in large ways. Each one can reset moments in time. As soon as you realize you made a mistake, embrace the cross. Repent. Take the hand of Jesus and let Him lead. God's love will restore you and everything that pertains to you. All things are possible for those who believe. Don't give up! Only believe! Humbling ourselves in submission to God through repentance is the ultimate act of obedience.

"Walk in obedience to all that the Lord your God has commanded you, so that you may live and prosper and prolong your days in the land that you will possess" (Deuteronomy 5:33, NIV). Every good and perfect gift comes from above, and He will not withhold good from those whose walk is right (Psalm 84:11). When we release our faith in obedience and obey His commands, He will continue to pour out His blessings on us repeatedly.

God rewards our obedience. Deuteronomy 28:1–14 gives us a clear picture of what God promises us when we are obedient to His commands. God blesses every area of our lives—our family, our children, our work, our health, and our income. When we keep the commands of the Lord our God and walk in His ways, people will know we are God's children because He blesses us with favor. Being blessed by God means God evokes His divine care in us.

When we obey the Lord, we can live a life of joy without shame. Walking in obedience to the Lord gives us the assurance that we are His children (1 John 2:3). As we continue to walk in obedience to the Lord, the areas of our lives we once found so difficult to overcome are no longer a struggle. As our lives transform into the likeness of Christ, we see our outlook on life change as we are looking more and more through His eyes.

> "You must love the Lord your God with all your heart, all your soul, and all your mind." This is the first and greatest commandment. A second is equally important: "Love your neighbor as yourself." The entire law and all

the demands of the prophets are based on these
two commandments.

Matthew 22:37–40 (NLT)

Pray Without Ceasing

Prayer is simply talking to God. Just as communication
in our marriages, with our children, in our workplace,
or in any relationship is vital to the growth, well-being,
knowledge, and understanding of that relationship, so is
our communication with God through prayer. Prayer is our
lifeline to the One who created us, to the source of our very
existence. Philippians 4:6 tells us not to be anxious about
anything, to pray about everything, to ask God for what we
need, and to thank Him for what He has done. Too often,
however, we do not think about prayer until something goes
very wrong and we are at the end of our rope.

Ask and you will receive, seek and you will find, knock
and the door will be opened to you (Matthew 7:7). Jesus
tells us whatever we ask in prayer, it will be given to us if

we ask in His name and believe it will be done (Matthew 21:21–22, John 14:13–14, John 16:24). The One who died for us (Jesus Christ) intercedes for us day and night (Romans 8:34). We are in partnership with Jesus and He who began a good work in us will complete it until the day we are with Him in heaven (Philippians 1:7).

When two or three are gathered together, there He is also (Matthew 18:20). Prayer is the release of faith. Faith releases God's perfect will. God's perfect will is His heart, which is found in His Word. God watches over His Word to see to it that His Word is fulfilled (Jeremiah 1:12). Ask God for whatever you wish (John 15:7). However, if we truly want God's best for us, and we truly want God's perfect plan for our lives to come into being, then we must be willing to trust God with what that should look like.

Prayer is not always talking. Prayer is listening to God too. When we are still and quiet before God, we will hear Him when He tells us the direction we should go or the decisions we should make. He already knows what is ahead. "The Lord will conquer your enemies when they attack you. They will attack you from one direction, but they will scatter from you in seven!" (Deuteronomy 28:7, NIV). This means God will make our enemies leave us completely, which is a completed work that is fully accomplished through the work Jesus Christ did on the cross of Calvary. This is God's covenant promise to us. When we humble ourselves before God, He will cause us to triumph over our enemies.

We pray for many things—healing, deliverance, salvation, needs, work and workplace, peace, hope, restoration of the good that has been lost, our families, our friends, and even those around the world we will never meet. Prayer shows our obedience to God in spending time caring for the needs of others, even when we are unable to physically help them ourselves. When we pray for the needs of others, we are asking God to move on their behalf and make sure their needs are met.

"There is one body and one Spirit—just as you were called to the one hope that belongs to your call—one Lord, one faith, one baptism, one God and Father of all, who is over all and through all and in all" (Ephesians 4:4–6, ESV). Even amidst our differences, as Christians, we are connected through Christ. Everything matters to the Lord. Everything should matter to us as well, and we should take all matters to the Lord in prayer.

"If my people, who are called by my name, will humble themselves and pray and seek my face and turn from their wicked ways, then I will hear from heaven, and I will forgive their sin and will heal their land" (2 Chronicles 7:14, NIV). This is God's command to His children. It has not changed over the span of thousands of years. We need God. Everything good comes from God. He will not withhold good from those whose walk is right. Prayer is still required for us to receive from the Lord those good things He has for us. Prayer will calm an anxious heart. Seeking our divine connection with God through prayer will soothe all doubts and calm all fears. Prayer is one way we let the Lord know we still look to Him first and put our faith in action that we trust He will do what He says He will do. "Trust in the Lord with all your heart" (Proverbs 3:5, ESV). Prayer speaks God's words into the atmosphere whereby the angels of God go forth to accomplish the word that God has spoken to bring change in our lives and in the lives of people around the world.

Sometimes, the prayers we pray seem to go unheard or unanswered. Daniel 10 describes Daniel praying and fasting for three weeks without receiving any indication his prayer had been heard. Daniel 10:13 lets us know Daniel's prayer had been heard, but the answer was delayed because a demonic force brought much resistance to the answer being fulfilled. Spiritual warfare is speaking God's Word into a situation against the demonic force sent to cause destruction against us or others. Then, through our authority in Christ, we speak God's Word of life into the same situation according to God's will. When we surrender to God's will, the Holy Spirit will lead us in how we should pray. God is in control. We must continue to stand firm and watch and pray.

There have been times I was so distraught I could not pray, not even for myself. I could not formulate an intelligent sentence to describe what I wanted and felt I needed from God. There were times when my soul was in so much anguish the only word I could say was "Jesus." God knows our thoughts, and He knows our hearts.

Romans 8:20–23 tells us even God's creation cries out to God to be restored to its former glory, free from death and decay. Certainly, God hears our cries, and He always knows what we need. When our thoughts are directed toward Him, He knows we are putting forth the effort to call out to Him. Even when we cannot say the words, God hears what our hearts are crying out for. He knows what every tear is unable to express in words. He not only hears those prayers, but He answers them too, for He is close to the brokenhearted.

Jesus is our perfect example. He is our advocate. While on the earth, He did not spread His message through violence. He spread His message of love and salvation with authority, and He prayed without ceasing. We cannot expect God to do everything that needs to be done. He will not do for us what He told us to do. We are in a relationship with Him. God put us on this earth to work and evoke change for the betterment of the world around us. Sometimes, we can feel we are being stretched farther than we are capable, but God says through Him, we are able. Wishing on a star will not bring everlasting results. These results will come through prayer. [17]

Time of Reflection

If you are willing and obedient, You shall eat the best of the land.

Isaiah 1:19 (AMP)

Describe an area of your life you want to see develop into a closer walk with the Lord.

Read John 10:4–5. Describe a time when you were not sure you heard God's voice give you direction.

Read Matthew 7:7 and Jeremiah 29:13. How will knowing God's promises affect your prayer life?

Take the time to pray and ask God to draw you closer to Him and help you hear Him clearly so you may follow Him in obedience.

Chapter 11

Walking with God Through Worship

Yet a time is coming and has now come when the true
worshipers will worship the Father in the Spirit and in
truth, for they are the kind of worshipers the Father seeks.
God is spirit, and his worshipers must worship in the Spirit
and in truth.

John 4:23–24 (NIV)

Worship with Your Time

There are many references in Scripture that talk about being good stewards of our time. He has made everything beautiful in its time. "He has also set eternity in the human heart" (Ecclesiastes 3:11, NIV). When we live our lives with an eternal purpose, we understand that everything on this earth will pass away (2 Corinthians 4:18), but eternity is forever. Time is a gift from God. We are to give God one-tenth of our increase. Our first increase is the time we are given each day (Genesis 28:22). Spending time with God and His Word each day before we rush out the door to do anything else gives our hearts and soul the fuel we need to renew, refresh, and energize, like eating breakfast gives our bodies the fuel we need to have the energy to start the day. When we give God the first fruits of our day, we will find the strength, assurance, and direction we need to accomplish the day set before us. "God's laws are pure, eternal, just. They are more desirable than gold. They are sweeter than honey dripping from a honeycomb" (Psalm 19:9–10, TLB).

"There is a time for everything, and a season for every activity under the heavens" (Ecclesiastes 3:1, NIV). Use your time wisely. "Be very careful, then, how you live—not as unwise but as wise, making the most of every opportunity, because the days are evil. Therefore do not be foolish, but understand what the Lord's will is" (Ephesians

5:15–17, NIV). Everyone needs to know they are not walking through this life alone. Take the time to spend some time with someone who doesn't have anyone close to them. Bringing a smile to the face of a lonely heart makes God smile.

Caring for all that God has entrusted to us includes spending time with our families. "Anyone who does not provide for their relatives, and especially for their own household, has denied the faith and is worse than an unbeliever" (1 Timothy 5:8, NIV). It is not difficult for many demands to take your attention away from the very ones you work to support. However, providing physical needs to your family is only part of what God expects from us. Our entire Christian walk revolves around relationships. Relationships are the very essence of our human existence. What our children see and hear us do, they will likely do.

> Oh, please, show the great power of your patience by forgiving our sins and showing us your steadfast love. Forgive us, even though you have said that you don't let sin go unpunished, and that you punish the father's fault in

the children to the third and fourth generation.

Numbers 14:18 (TLB)

The consequences of the sin of the parents can fall upon the children, as children are a product of how they are raised. The mistakes of the parents are often repeated by their children—sometimes for many generations. This is the root of why we see the breakdown in our families and, ultimately, in our society. When our families break down, the essence of our society breaks down because society is made of interactions through human relationships. Spend time with your children. Show interest in their interests. Show interest in their concerns. Show them you will always be there for them and love them unconditionally. "Direct your children onto the right path, and when they are older, they will not leave it" (Proverbs 22:6, NLT). As a Christian, the right path should be in the knowledge and admonition of the Lord. "Fathers, do not provoke your children to anger by the way you treat them. Rather, bring them up with the discipline and instruction that comes from the Lord"

(Ephesians 6:4, NLT).

Hebrews 10:25 admonishes us not to neglect meeting together in the great assembly, meaning we need to attend regular worship services with our brothers and sisters in Christ and encourage one another. When we fail to do so, we are robbing ourselves of growing stronger spiritually and growing stronger in a relationship with one another. One prayer Jesus Himself prayed while He was on this earth was for Christians to walk in unity with one another, just as Jesus and God are one with each other. This is the desire of God's heart. Even with the diversity of denominations, races, cultures, and generations, as Christians, we are all clay molded by the same potter: our Lord and Savior, Jesus Christ. When we stand together, united in Christ, we see the walls of division and strife in our church, our homes, our communities, our nation, and around the world come down. When we do not regularly attend worship services and do not stand united as one body in Christ Jesus, we become like a sitting duck—we remove ourselves from the covering of protection God gives us through worshipping together in a church community. Worship the Lord in spirit and truth.

Worship with Tithes and Offerings

Worship is an outward reaction to God because of the inward change that has occurred in us. Giving the first fruits of our income is an act of obedience to a command of God. "Honor the Lord with your wealth and with the first fruits of all your crops (income); Then your barns will be abundantly filled And your vats will overflow with new wine" (Proverbs 3:9–10, AMP). Malachi 3:10 (AMP) says,

> "Bring all the tithes (the tenth) into the storehouse, so that there may be food in My house, and test Me now in this," says the Lord of hosts, "if I will not open for you the windows of heaven and pour out for you [so great] a blessing until there is no more room to receive [contain] it."

In verse 11, God tells us when we do, He will cause us to prosper. "Give, and it will be given to you. Good measure, pressed down, shaken together, running over, will be put into your lap. For with the measure you use it will be measured back to you" (Luke 6:38, ESV). God knows our hearts. He knows our motives. "You must each decide in your heart how much to give. And don't give reluctantly or in response to pressure. 'For God loves a person who gives cheerfully'" (2 Corinthians 9:7, NLT).

Giving our tithe is our way of giving thanks to God and acknowledging to Him that we know He is our source for everything good we have, even our income. "Everything comes from you, and we have given you only what comes from your hand" (1 Chronicles 29:14, NIV). We honor God when we demonstrate our continued understanding that God is Jehovah Jireh, our provider, even down to the last penny and the last second of time.

I was blessed to be born to a mother who loves the Lord and honored Him faithfully with tithes and offerings. I distinctly remember the conversation we had when she taught me the importance of tithing. My mother and father both worked while we were growing up. They worked hard for all they had, and though there were times when we barely had enough, my mother continued to tithe to their church. She told me there was a time when she felt they could not pay their bills if she gave tithes. She described how, after discontinuing tithes, even after taking on extra work, they still did not have enough money to take care of all the family's financial responsibilities. After learning this lesson, she never again withheld giving their tithe to God. She told me when she was faithful to the Lord in tithing, we never experienced lack or need, and our bills were always paid on time. She said, "I do not know how it works, but it does." God is faithful. When we are obedient to the Lord, He honors us.

During my own walk with the Lord, I have experienced the same. I have never forgotten that lesson my mother taught me, and I continue to honor the Lord with the first fruits of my income even today. The Lord also taught me that honoring God also means honoring those through whom I receive spiritual nourishment and giving to people and ministries. When we are obedient to give as God tells us to give, God will always give back to us and more than we can think, ask, or imagine. In our giving offerings to support people and ministries, we "give to the Lord the glory he deserves! Bring your offering and come into

His courts. Worship the Lord in all his holy splendor. Let all the earth tremble before him" (Psalm 96:8–9, NLT). "Honor the Lord with your wealth and with the best part of everything you produce. Then He will fill your barns with grain, and your vats will overflow with good wine" (Proverbs 3:9–10, NLT). God tells us not to give reluctantly or out of compulsion (2 Corinthians 9:7) but that "every man shall give as he is able, according to the blessing of the Lord your God that he has given you" (Deuteronomy 16:17, ESV). God is faithful. The blessing of the Lord brings wealth and riches and adds no sorrow to it (Proverbs 10:22).

Worship with Your Body, Mind, and Soul

"Let all that I am praise the Lord; with my whole heart, I will praise his holy name…may I never forget the good things he does for me" (Psalm 103:1–2, NLT). God did not make His covenant with us to be on a part-time or limited basis. He made His covenant with us, and He gives us His best. In return, He wants us to give Him our best. Love the Lord with all your heart, soul, and strength (Deuteronomy

6:5).

> For God, who said, "Let light shine out of darkness," made his light shine in our hearts to give us the light of the knowledge of God's glory displayed in the face of Christ. But we have this treasure in jars of clay to show that this all-surpassing power is from God and not from us.

2 Corinthians 4:6–7 (NIV)

Our bodies are the vessels through which God chooses to reside and our lives through which God chooses to show His glory to the world. If we do not do what is within our ability to take care of the bodies God has given us, we are taking for granted what God has blessed us with. This may not only cause pain and hardship for us, but it may also lessen our days with which to make an eternal difference in the lives of others.

"He himself has said, 'You must be holy, for I am holy'" (1 Peter 1:16, TLB).

Let us behave decently, as in the daytime, not in carousing and drunkenness, not in sexual immorality and debauchery [excessive indulgence in things that satisfy the desires of the flesh], not in dissension and jealousy. Rather, clothe yourselves with the Lord Jesus Christ, and do not think about how to gratify the desires of the flesh.

Romans 13:13–14 (NIV)

Maintain healthy relationships and allow God to cut unhealthy ties that serve to weigh you down and drain your soul. Allow Him to cleanse you and make you whole.

God gave me a vision that sent me to the floor on my face. Stunning, miraculous, and I will never forget what He showed me. Jesus was standing in front of me with His back to me. He turned to His right, which caused me to see the right profile side of His body. From within Him came a person who I had been praying for, who was clothed in the exact same clothing as Jesus. This person was stepping out of the very essence of Jesus' whole body. I melted.

When we clothe ourselves with Jesus Christ, or as Scripture says, put on Christ (Romans 13:14), we are putting on the indispensable qualities of who Christ is in heart and mind. This showed me a very clear picture of what living a life in Christ means. This is who God desires us to be. We can do so when we worship Him with all our heart, body, mind, and soul. "So all of us who have had that veil removed can see and reflect the glory of the Lord. And the Lord—who is the Spirit—makes us more and more like him as we are changed into his glorious image" (2 Corinthians 3:18, NLT). If we love God, we will want to know Him better. True worship will draw us closer to God and help us overcome the effects of the world.

Worship through Our Choices

The purpose of our worship is to bring honor and glory to God and to show Him we love Him. What does it say about us if after we come to God with a broken and contrite heart, confessing our need for a Savior and repenting before Him to receive His forgiveness of our sins, then turn around and continue to make choices that do not reflect that change we say we have experienced from within? God sees our hearts. "For you created my inmost being; you knit me together in my mother's womb" (Psalm 139:13, NIV). "Humble yourselves before the Lord, and he will lift you up in honor" (James 4:6, 10, NLT). With the Spirit of the Living God within us, we can live life no longer bound by the things of this world. We are to work out our salvation with fear and trembling. God tells us to choose. When we choose to worship God in a way that He determines is acceptable, we will reap great benefits.

I have heard it said, "You can't be my friend if you can't be my friend." Ralph Waldo Emerson was quoted as saying, "The only way to have a friend is to be one."[18]

Suppose you have a friend who has been your friend since childhood. This friend has stood by you and stood up for you in the face of bullies time and time again. Through high school, college, and marriage, this friend has been faithful to support you and hold you up even during your most painful moments. From out of nowhere, but in the normal course of events of daily life, others come into your life trying to be your best friend. Do you now cast aside the person who has been your life-long friend and act as if you never knew them? Do we do this to Jesus? The answer is yes; too often, we do. After all Jesus Christ has done for us, how could we let ourselves get caught up in other people or circumstances, giving them our central focus and attention and putting our Savior on a shelf?

God called Abraham a friend (Isaiah 41:8). When we become Christians, God calls us friends.

> You are my friends if you do what I command. I no longer call you slaves, because a master doesn't confide in his slaves. Now you are my friends, since I have told you everything the Father told me. You didn't choose me. I chose you. I appointed you to go and produce lasting fruit, so that the Father will give you whatever you ask for, using my name.

> John 15:14–16 (NLT)

Remember the day you called Him Lord and asked Him for the many things you wanted and needed? He was the faithful friend who came and stood by your side and rescued you each time. "Look! I have been standing at the door, and I am constantly knocking. If anyone hears me calling him and opens the door, I will come in and fellowship with him and he with me" (Revelation 3:20, TLB).

When we do not worship God with our choices, we will slowly drift away from God. It happens subtly. Not that we ever intend for it to happen, but it can still happen. When we choose what the world has to offer over what God wants to give us, we become what God plainly says in James 4:4 (NIV): "You adulterous people, don't you know that friendship with the world means enmity against God? Therefore, anyone who chooses to be a friend of the world becomes an enemy of God." "Walk with the wise and become wise; associate with fools and get in trouble" (Proverbs 13:20, NLT). We are known by the company we keep. "One who has unreliable friends soon comes to ruin, but there is a friend who sticks closer than a brother" (Proverbs 18:24, NIV). When you realize you are not where God wants you to be, turn your actions around and follow Christ. God is loving, merciful, and forgiving with a grace that knows no bounds.

When we come into a relationship with God, He likens the relationship to a marriage, wherein a covenant is made between Him and the new believer in Christ. A new believer in Christ tells God they trust Him to save their soul. God tells the new believers He trusts them to live a life that reflects His love. Marriage, as in any relationship, is built on trust. When a person turns and begins to make choices that do not reflect that trust, a breach occurs and threatens the strength of the marriage. The same is true in our relationship with God. God tells us that turning away from keeping Him first causes a break in the trust covenant between us and God. How can a good God who is loving, kind, merciful, and gracious say this? Because God is also holy and He is righteous. God is also truth, and He cannot deny it. He cannot and will not overlook sin. God loves us, and He wants His best for us. He has given us His Son so that the world would know He is mighty to save so that they will come to Him and repent before it is too late and time has run out! It is that simple.

Living a life loving God and putting Him first does not mean we are to close ourselves off to the world we live in. We will continue to work, go to school, shop for our families, and interact in our communities. God asks us not to conform to the ways of the world in our thoughts or in the way we live. He knows how hard this can be, especially when relationships are based on the expectations of how we live. He asks us to live in such a way that our choices will reflect our relationship with Him. Seek God. Stay in communication with Him. He will not ignore you. He will not let you down. He gave His best for us, and in return, He asks us to love Him completely. Jesus said, "So, because you are lukewarm—neither hot nor cold—I am about to spit you out of my mouth" (Revelation 3:16, NIV). There will come a day of reckoning. There will come a day when everyone who has ever lived will stand face to face with God and answer for everything they have ever done. When that day comes, what will be said about your life and the choices you have made?

God tells us, "Now listen! Today I am giving you a choice between life and death, between prosperity and disaster…Oh, that you would choose life, so that you and your descendants might live…And if you love and obey the Lord, you will live long in the land the Lord swore to give you" (Deuteronomy 30:15, 19–20, NLT). We are responsible for caring for and managing all God gives us, whether it is time, choices, tithes and offerings, or gifts and talents. Choose Life! Choose to have a heart of worship[19]

Time of Reflection

I will bless the Lord at all times; His praise shall continually be in my mouth.

Psalm 34:1 (AMP)

What does worshipping God mean to you?

Read 1 Chronicles 29:14. How will this affect what you give to God, whether in money, time, or the gifts He has given you?

Read John 4:23–24 and Psalm 145:18. What does this mean to you?

Take the time to pray and ask God to stir you up to worship Him in spirit and in truth in such a way that is honoring to Him.

Chapter 12

Walk in His Light

For at one time you were darkness, but now you are light in the Lord. Walk as children of light.

Ephesians 5:8 (ESV)

The Light of His Truth

As we have studied, walking in the light of the Lord is not as simple as someone saying, "Now walk as children of light." There are many aspects to be considered, weighed, and understood for us to complete a successful walk with Christ on this earth. Our lives are like a jigsaw puzzle with pieces put together through life experiences, torn apart through brokenness, and restored again by God's love and grace. Isaiah 11 tells us that through Christ, God gives us a spirit of knowledge, understanding, and wisdom, His Spirit that gives power and might, a reverent fear (respect) of God, and submission in obedience to His Holy Spirit. Throughout the course of this book, we have embarked on the knowledge that creates the basic recipe of what we need to understand so we can successfully walk in the light of Christ's salvation.

As infants, we are taught how to crawl. After that new adventurous level of growth has been attained, we venture further to take the first step. Though wobbling and unsure, the drive in our spirit tells us not to give up and to keep trying. Soon, we find we no longer need to hold on to something or someone to walk. We are gliding across the floor with increased ease. Before you know it, we are racing across the floor with newfound discoveries that keep us hungry for more. We find endless possibilities through the challenges we face along the way. Occasionally, we look back and see from where we have traveled and realize we really can achieve anything we set our minds to do. Navigating through our lives in this world is much the same. In our relationship with the Lord, we grow with Him step by step.

When we tie together every lesson outlined in this book, we realize in God's unrelenting love for His children that He painstakingly guides us through achieving knowledge and understanding so we may walk in wisdom against the forces in this world set against us. To take only part of God's Word to heart and not accept and receive all of God's truth is a great injustice to oneself.

I remember a time when the struggles in my life were so clouded by every firing missile aimed at me that I found myself unable to process the progressive thoughts and emotions weighing against my soul. Each time I had what seemed an impossible moment, I would pick up the phone and call someone to talk about it. One day, as I met with this dilemma, every attempt I made to call someone ended with no one answering their phone. The Lord spoke to me and said, "Ask Me." This word began my journey of discovery that has taken me on a great adventure into new life and has rescued my soul, restored my mind, and brought healing to a level I never imagined was possible.

This is the love of Abba Father for His children. This

is our Father in heaven, who wants to be involved in every part of your life, who will never turn you away, who never thinks your questions are too dumb to ask, and who knows your troubles are never too difficult to work out. This is God, the Creator of the heavens and earth, who sees everything good and bad about you and still wants to have a close relationship with you so much that He sent His only Son who was willing to leave the splendor of heaven, come to earth and give His own life for you so that you can live for eternity with Him in heaven. This is the one true God who gave us His Word with instructions to navigate through all life's challenges. In the past, I put my trust and hope in other things, all of which failed with great intensity. God has never failed to keep what He promised to me.

Trust and Obey

God's Word is the inexhaustible source that reveals the great mysteries deep into God's heart and illuminates this great treasure in our souls. Put God's Word in your heart, seek Him for understanding, and He will guide your steps. Success at every level in our walk with Christ depends on our willingness to accept His Word and ways as truth. "Sovereign Lord, you are God! Your covenant is trustworthy, and you have promised these good things to your servant" (2 Samuel 7:28, NIV). Remember that worship means honoring God as the most important person in our lives. Give God first place in your life. Choose your words carefully. Understand life and death lie in what you say. If you slip or fall, do not beat yourself up; simply confess it and repent right away. Know God is for us and not against us, and He is faithful to forgive us and make everything right once again.

Do not repay evil with evil. Pray for mercy and grace for others because you will surely need it yourself one day. If we decide to give up, bow out, or completely turn away from the Christian faith based on perceptions, another's perspective, misdeeds, or any other reason would be the greatest travesty of injustice. How can we possibly achieve salvation based on the example of imperfection? There is only one viable solution to find true rest for the troubled soul. Look to the One who created all things and is perfect in every way to find the example of how we should live and seek only friendship from all others. Ultimately, the choice is ours. We must each work out our own salvation with fear and trembling, and it should never depend on others. When we meet with God face to face, He will not ask us about what someone else did or did not do; He will only ask us how we lived the life he gave us.

For some, trusting someone you cannot see who promises life, love, and victory can be a daunting task. It should bring great comfort in knowing God chooses you and chooses to use you. He makes us who we are through His power working in us. Trust Him to bring it to completion. Commit your heart to the One who has engraved your name in His hand—the One who is able to keep your foot from slipping. Never forget that even when we face difficult times, we never face them alone. God will never leave us or forsake us. The Lord God Almighty is He who is faithful and true. Praise His holy name!

Decide for Yourself

In the vast ocean of souls on this earth, I am only one person. Honestly, knowing the suffering of others makes my troubles seem pale in comparison. I have, however, come to know that God does not hold any one person as more important than another. My achievements, desires, sorrows, and setbacks are just as important to God as anyone else's. The same is true for everyone. I have found God to be faithful, gracious, loving, kind, and merciful to me all along the way, giving me peace when nothing made sense. In my service to the Lord, He has always come to my defense when others mistook my mission because He is my defender. If you are not sure about His nature, His promises, or His purpose, ask Him to make Himself real to you and make clear His purpose. When you do, be sure you are ready to hear it because He will surely do it! Decide for yourself. God's eternal word is truth. He is the Alpha and Omega, the beginning and the end. He is I Am That I Am from now until the very end.

All Is Well with My Soul

We all come to a place in our lives when we realize we are not living in this world alone. Not one is alike. Not everyone was raised with the same beliefs, and some people, in all the days of their lives, have never known peace. Anytime we read the headlines or newsfeeds, we hear of injustices plaguing the world we live in. In fact, the Lord tells us we will face troubles in this world. At the same time, He tells us not to fear and not to worry because He has overcome the world. It seems unattainable to obtain this peace God gives, this peace that passes all understanding, especially when you experience the loss of a loved one, a family member, or a child whose life ended too early. Many walk with hopelessness and despair after losing their only source of income, and then they endure the loss of their homes and all their possessions. Too many innocent lives fall victim to the hate in the darkness of this world, as they are shamelessly violated or killed, and many will find no justice because of the level of insanity of disregard with no repentance in this world.

The Lord told us there would be difficult seasons in our lives on this earth—bad things happen to good people. But He also promised He would never leave us or forsake us. He promised us He would walk by our sides throughout every struggle, through every tear, through every lonely moment, through every doubt, throughout every season.

So how, in this world of darkness, is anyone able to walk in the light of God's salvation? Understand that there will always be injustices in this world while sin and evil are present, but in God's holy presence, grace abounds. The light of His salvation is seen through those who choose to believe in Jesus as their personal Lord and Savior and will allow the light of His truth to shine through them in how they live. Jesus is the light, and through Him comes salvation and life everlasting in heaven. Jesus is the life, and in Him we have life and live in God's holy presence. Given the light of His truth, may it be said of you that all is well with your soul.

We Live in His Grace

Even amidst life's uncertainties, you can find peace and contentment in the soul-saving, life-changing power of Jesus Christ the King. I know I have. Though my journey has encompassed many life changes and covered the span of many current events, He has never let me down. I cannot say I never had a doubt. There have been times I wondered if I would complete His plan and purpose. At my lowest point, after being snared by sin's deception, I asked God if I had exhausted my grace account, to which He replied, "It's just going to be harder." In the worst of it all, God never turned me away, and He never let me go. When God calls you to do something, He doesn't change His mind, and He will always confirm His Word. He will fulfill His plan and purpose in our lives as long as we do not say no. I have learned that even through all the ups and downs, life with Christ has far surpassed my wanderings without Him. His unconditional love and acceptance of me have set me free. I felt His love for me so strong it was consuming. If I could give anyone a glimpse into what the Lord has taught me during my passage through this land, it would be to listen to the words of wisdom from the Lord, seek His best for your life, and never settle for less. Settling for less than His best will cost you more than you would ever want to pay.

Of the immeasurable treasures He has taught me, this I share with you: "Hold unswervingly to the hope we profess, for he who promised is faithful" (Hebrews 10:23, NIV). Even amid every storm and the fires that sweep across our lands with malice of intent, it is God who picks us up, carries us, and makes us able to stand firm in Him.

A house divided against itself is doomed. Even with our differences, stand united in one spirit, one mind, and in one accord against the one who comes to steal, kill, and destroy. Refuse to take offense and do not allow yourself to be deceived, for not everything is as it seems. When we stand united, we will be amazed by the positive turn of events in this world. Many walk away from church because of the condition of unrest that arises when we do not stand united in the body of Christ. We must all do our part to bridge the great divide.

Do not become distraught if agents of the enemy come against you. Stand and take authority against them. God will defend and care for you. Look what God did to Moab, who, without repentance, mocked and ridiculed the children of Israel for their misfortune. Now Moab is stricken from existence (Jeremiah 48). By the same token, do not gloat over someone's misfortune or presume you know why it has happened. Give grace and not harshness, but for the grace of God, it could have easily been you.

God's Word to His church is decisive. Lift Him up, and all men will be drawn to Him. Realize God's favor surrounds us like a shield. Praise the Lord, for God inhabits the praises of His children. Praise the Lord when things go well and put the devil in His place. Praise the Lord when things are tough because this will confuse Satan and render him powerless to succeed against you. There is power in the name of Jesus!

It is for the glory of God to conceal a matter and the heart of kings to search it out. Christ has made us kings and priests who serve before God His Father (Revelation 1:6). We are the kings who are to search out those great mysteries. God tells us that when we ask Him, He will answer us and show us great and mighty things that will reveal His heart (Jeremiah 33:3). It is to our credit and for our benefit when we accept what God gives us. As a child of God, we hold within us the hidden treasure of the great kingdom of God. Nothing can separate us from God's love, and nothing in this world is worth losing your place in heaven!

Take Jesus with you wherever you go, in your heart,

your mind, and soul. Allow God room to work in a situation. He will work it out, either by changing you or someone else, but He will always judge in your favor. Walk with the courage of Daniel as he stood amongst the lions and with the unwavering faith of young King David as he faced Goliath. Do not doubt God's power, for even three young Hebrew boys went through the fire, came out alive, and did not smell of smoke. Joshua never backed down in the face of a fight and watched God bring the walls of Jericho down. He saw God's favor time and time again and determined that he and his house would serve the Lord. It is in our weaknesses that God's strength shines.

Keep your eyes focused on God's best, and do not quit in the face of discouragement. We are not measured by our failures but by God's holiness. We cannot fail if we do not give up. Be determined to think positively and believe that God will cause you to triumph and prosper and limit your time with those who do not think the same.

Tell the voice of regret to go because if you do not, this will only serve to bury you in discouragement. God has your best interest at heart, just as He does for everyone in all creation. Make God's Word your rule and reject the lies that only serve to suck the life out of you. Thank God for new beginnings—this brings newness to life. Every day with Jesus is a new day to try again to get it right.

Living life in this world can be difficult and very trying at times. Many choices and belief systems are offered by the spirit of man and the spirit of the world, but through Christ Jesus and the Spirit of God, we are equipped to walk in the light of His salvation. You may get discouraged, but a harvest of blessings will come if you do not give up. Your walk was never intended to look like anyone else's, so do not compare their success to yours. God does not show favoritism. He has a great blessing in store for you; just believe. Be willing to learn and have a teachable spirit, for there is always room to grow. Enjoy the good He gives you. God says you are worth it!

We are all a part of God's unique design and His perfect plan—keep moving forward. Purpose in your heart to laugh every day. Doing so will decrease stress, increase healing, and even reduce pain. One of my greatest joys has been to see a smile on the face of a lonely soul after sharing time with them. Allow God to use you wherever you go.

God's thoughts and His love are far above anything we can think or imagine. Do not rely on yourself; take His hand and let Him lead, and know there is safety in the council of many. Following Jesus is not impossible. He will give you what you need. Trust God in His truth. Good comes from His hand. If it doesn't come from Jesus, you don't need it!

May this be your story, and may the testimony spread that your soul has finally found peace. And on that great day when Jesus returns, may you be found sitting at His feet.

Time of Reflection

The Lord will fulfill his purpose for me; Your steadfast love,

O Lord, endures forever.

Psalm 138:8 (ESV)

List three things you learned from reflecting on God's Word as outlined in this book.

Discuss three ways this book has helped you better understand how you can walk in the light of God's salvation.

Take the time to pray and ask God to help you to stay mindful of His presence in your life and, in all things, choose life.

Prayer to Receive Christ as Savior

For "Everyone who calls on the name of the Lord
will be saved."

Romans 10:13 (NLT)

The Word of God says if you confess with your mouth that Jesus is Lord and believe in your heart that God raised Him from the dead, you will be saved (Romans 10:9). It is that simple. I invite you to say the following prayer of faith to become a believer in Christ:

Lord, I know I am a sinner in need of a Savior. I ask you to forgive my sins and be the Lord of my life. In Jesus' name. Amen.

When we confess our sins, God is faithful and just to forgive us of our sins and cleanse us of all unrighteousness (1 John 1:9). To make our walk with Christ successful, it is vitally important to stay connected to a local Bible teaching church in your area. Get a Bible and start reading it every day. Take the time to be still and allow God to speak to you through it. You will be amazed to find out how much the Lord really loves you when you take the time to get to know Him.

About the Author

Katrina Stanley is a mother of two adult children and has three grandchildren. She is a minister, writer, singer, songwriter, and speaker and has served as a worship pastor. She has served in local pregnancy resource centers and is an advocate for the sanctity of life. She co-facilitated *Living Free*, a program designed to set people free from life-controlling issues. In her ministry, Katrina Stanley Ministries, she shares how God brought her through the difficult journey of recovery after many difficult seasons. Her passion is to see the broken and hurting come into the light of God's truth and love that will set them free. She encourages people to "Never give up. There is always hope!" You can find Katrina online at www.katrinastanley.org, on Facebook, and on YouTube.

Endnotes

[1] Katrina Stanley, *In His Grace,* (2006)

[2] Billy Graham, *The Reason for My Hope* (Nashville, TN: W. Publishing, 2013).

[3] Wikipedia, "Walter Scott," last modified November 28, 2023, https://en.wikipedia.org/wiki/Walter_Scott.

[4] Katrina Stanley, "Katrina Stanley--Love Always Performed at An Evening With Kay Warren on 03 13 2015," YouTube, posted November 9, 2015, www.youtube.com/watch?v=qwVjyXJcnHs.

[5] Kenneth E. Hagin, *The Believer's Authority* (Tulsa, OK: Kenneth Hagin Ministries, 1996).

[6] Joseph Prince, *Destined to Reign* (Tulsa, OK: Harrison House Publishers, 2007).

[7] Joel Osteen, *The Power of I Am* (Nashville, TN: FaithWords, 2015).

[8] Wikipedia, "The best defense is a good offense," last modified June 19, 2023, https://en.wikipedia.org/wiki/The_best_defense_is_a_good_offense.

[9] John Ramirez, *Unmasking The Devil* (Shippensburg, PA: Destiny Image Publishers, 2015).

[10] Robert Henderson, *Operating in the Courts of Heaven* (Robert Henderson Ministries, 2014).

[11] Wikipedia, "Facing The Giants," last modified November 19, 2023, https://en.wikipedia.org/wiki/Facing_the_Giants.

[12] Joyce Meyer, *Battlefield of the Mind: Winning the Battle in Your Mind* (New York, NY: FaithWords Publishing, 2008).

[13] Kay Warren, *Choose Joy* (Grand Rapids, MI: Revell, 2012).

[14] Juliette Hall Byam, *Forgiveness: What's the Big Deal*

(USA: Xulon Press, 2016).

[15] Perry Stone, *Opening the Gates of Heaven* (Lake Mary, FL: Charisma House, 2012).

[16] Priscilla Shirer, *Discerning The Voice of God* (Chicago, IL: Moody Publishers, 2012).

[17] Mark Batterson, *The Circle Maker* (Grand Rapids, MI: Zondervan, 2011).

[18] AZquotes, "Ralph Waldo Emerson quote The only way to have a friend is to be one," accessed December 5, 2023, https://azquotes.com/quote/89251.

[19] Chuck D. Pierce and John Dickson, *Worship As It Is in Heaven* (Ventura, CA: Regal Books, 2010).